Shadows of the Heart

Books by the Whiteheads

SHADOWS OF THE HEART

A *Spirituality of* *the Painful Emotions*

James D. Whitehead
AND
Evelyn Eaton Whitehead

A Crossroad Book

CROSSROAD · NEW YORK

1996
The Crossroad Publishing Company
370 Lexington Avenue, New York, NY 10017

Printed in the United States of America

Grateful acknowledgment is made for use of material from "The Field Pansy" from *Westward* by
Amy Clampitt, Copyright © 1990 by Amy Clampitt, reprinted by permission of Alfred A. Knopf
Inc.; for use of "Ten Commandments of the Negative Traditional Core" from *When Feeling Bad
is Good* by Ellen McGrath, Copyright © 1992 by Ellen McGrath, reprinted by permission of
Henry Holt and Company, Inc.; for use of material from "Until Now" by Joe Kogel, Copyright
© 1989 by Joe Kogel, reprinted by permission of the author; and for use of the following material
by James D. Whitehead and Evelyn Eaton Whitehead which appeared previously: "Christians
and Their Passions," *Review for Religious* (September/October, 1993); "Guilt: Is It a Blessing or
a Curse?" *Sisters Today* (July 1992); "Good Guilt / Bad Guilt," *Inform: Current Thinking on Catholic
Issues* (January 1992).

All scriptural quotations are taken from *The New Revised Standard Version* (London: Collins,
1989), unless otherwise noted. JB indicates a quotation taken from *The Jerusalem Bible* (New
York: Doubleday. 1968).

Library of Congress Cataloging-in-Publication Data

Whitehead, James D.
    Shadows of the heart : a spirituality of the painful emotions /
James D. Whitehead and Evelyn Eaton Whitehead.
        p.   cm.
    Includes bibliographical references and index.
    ISBN 0-8245-1441-6; 0-8245-1534-X (pbk.)
    1. Spiritual life.   2. Emotions—Religious aspects—Christianity.
3. Anger—Religious aspects—Christianity.   4. Shame—Religious
aspects—Christianity.   5. Guilt—Religious aspects—Christianity.
6. Christian life.   I. Whitehead, Evelyn Eaton.   II. Title.
233'.5—dc20   94-18087
                                                                    CIP

For family

Joan Eaton McSweeney
Robert Eaton
Evie Eaton Dunkelberger
Fernin Eaton
Marie Eaton de Verges

Acknowledgments

First thanks go to our longtime colleague and companion, James R. Zullo, for all we have learned from him in seminars on the negative emotions the three of us have offered together. His good counsel has shaped this project from its beginning. To the women religious at our workshop in Orange County, California, ten years ago, whose strong feelings initially spurred our study of negative emotions: This book is the fruit of your anger. Early on, William G. Thompson suggested we include the emotion of shame in our study; Bill's advice has borne fruit again and again.

Our friends Michael Cowan and Bernard Lee, in lively discussions over several years, helped clarify and refine our perspective. We thank them especially for their firm encouragement to keep our gaze on the social as well as the personal dynamics of emotional life.

We thank Denise Carmody and John Carmody for their kind offer to join them at the Warren Center for Catholic Studies at the University of Tulsa during the fall semester of 1992. This opportunity to work with their diverse student body and with the ministry students of Phillips Seminary expanded our approach. The Carmodys' greatest gift to us, though, has been the grace of their friendship during this privileged time.

To all our colleagues at the Institute of Pastoral Studies at Loyola University in Chicago, our enduring gratitude. The Institute has been for us for twenty-five years an enriching "holding environment"—a safe place to raise challenging questions, an abode of critical and generous faith. To the participants in our workshops and courses on the negative emotions, at IPS and elsewhere, we acknowledge a particular debt: Your wisdom, candor, and practical support have enlivened both these writers and our work.

To Sister Mary O. Lam, MIC of Good Hope School, Father George Zee, S.J. of the Whole Person Centre, and the participants in our 1994 workshop in Hong Kong we offer special thanks for the opportunity to test our understandings of anger, patience, and shame in so stimulating a crosscultural setting.

On the home front, we are blessed with lively companions who have survived endless dinner conversations on anger, guilt, shame, and depression. Mary Ulrich, Catherine LaCugna, Gene Ulrich, Patty Hackett, Ann and Gordy Myers—we salute your passionate endurance. We dedicate this book to Evelyn's five brothers and sisters, who embody the special emotional energy that is the signature of the Eaton family.

J.D.W. and E.E.W.
February 25, 1994

Contents

Part Four

Transforming Our Passions

Conclusion

Part One

THE GOOD NEWS
ABOUT BAD FEELINGS

The Chinese character for patience (jen)
shows a knife poised over a heart:
the willingness to hold still, in painful settings,
until we know what we are feeling

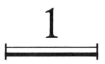

1

Emotions—Unlikely Allies

An emotion is a transformation of the world.
Jean-Paul Sartre

To be human is to be aroused. Emotion ignites our best behaviors: courage in the face of danger, a fierce attachment to our children, the anger that resists injustice. Our emotions also impel us to our worst excesses: violent rage, sexual abuse, corrosive guilt. If we can hardly live with our distressing feelings, we cannot live without them. In their absence, we may survive for a while, but we will not thrive.

The Puzzle of Feelings

"The fact was I didn't feel much of anything very cleanly or purely, if that makes any sense. It was as if I had been churned up inside, so that all my emotions were colored with one another and had become one muddy shade." A teenager in Richard Bausch's novel *Rebel Powers* reminds us how perplexing emotions are. Uneasiness leaves us upset and confused, but what are we feeling? A surge of indignation goads us to take action; but what's the best way to respond? Or, unexpectedly, joy floods our heart; where does this surprising contentment spring from? In the chapters ahead we will explore the puzzle of emotion. Our focus is on the negative feelings of anger, guilt, shame, and depression.

What do we mean by "negative" emotions? Some emotions make us feel wretched. Anger's racing pulse sets us on edge. Shame taunts us with messages of our unworthiness. Guilt's recriminations preoccupy and dishearten us. Depression drains all delight from our life.

And beyond the bad feelings within, these emotions have distressing consequences. Anger's fury can ignite violence and injury. Shame and guilt feed addictive behavior, as people seek relief—unsuccessfully—in the momentary high of drugs or sex or food. Depression weakens the immune system, shrinking our stamina and leaving us vulnerable to other illnesses.

Negative cultural messages reinforce these personal experiences. Conventional psychoanalysis links depression with neurosis; self-help gurus insist that guilt is immature. Anger makes religion's list of "seven deadly sins." And most discussions of shame cite it as a wound to be healed, the toxic residue of childhood abuse, a hidden dynamic in a host of harmful behaviors.

Under the weight of these negative assessments, we learn to link these emotions to inadequacy and weakness. Soon we *feel bad about feeling bad*. Whenever guilt arises or anger stirs, the inner judgment automatically sounds: "I should not be feeling like this!" Embarrassed by our negative emotions, we make haste to banish them. But banishing bad feelings seldom works.

Why Look at the Negative Emotions

The drive to understand negative emotions starts in personal need. All of us have been caught up in emotion's turmoil. Bewildered by some internal upheaval, we try to make sense of what is happening to us. If we are to live satisfying and fruitful lives, we know we must come to terms with these powerful forces.

And the need touches the public world as well. Recent studies have uncovered the code of silence that encourages health professionals and other caregivers to ignore their feelings of sadness and grief. "Our profession has always been about helping others, and our needs have traditionally been lost in the shuffle," a spokesperson for the American Association of Critical-Care Nurses reports. "The tension between the grief that many professionals feel and the implicit code of silence their jobs demand often causes emotional and physical suffering." A nurse working with cancer patients adds, "Being professional has always meant this macho, stoic capacity to swallow everything." An inability to acknowledge the emotional distress that accompanies their work leads many human service professionals into burnout and exhaustion. Some highly trained practitioners leave the field. Others develop psychological defenses—cynicism, emotional withdrawal—that diminish their effectiveness and erode their commitment to the work. From both mental health and economic perspectives, learning better ways to deal with painful feelings becomes imperative.

Social research uncovers even more compelling concerns about negative emotions. In their analysis of sexual addictions in *Lonely All the Time*, psychologists Ralph Earle and Gregory Crow show the link between addiction and unmanageable negative emotions. Research on sexual violence finds that "rapists often recall being intensely angry, depressed or feeling worthless for days or even months leading up to the rape." A study of patterns of feeling, thought, and action among child molesters notes that "the cycle begins with feelings like anger or intense loneliness and depression."

Reports on drug use makes similar connections between negative emotions and addictive behavior. Although many adolescents experiment with alcohol and illegal drugs, only a small percentage develop debilitating drug habits that continue into adulthood. Social scientists wanted to know why. They found the primary difference was how young persons handled their negative emotions. Adolescents who used drugs primarily to get rid of bad feelings were more likely to accelerate their use over time. Many of these teens became seriously addicted adults. In contrast, young people who developed effective ways to deal with or move beyond bad feelings tended to give up drugs altogether or limit their use to social occasions. Here again, learning how to deal with negative emotions is the key.

The negative emotions raise special questions for religious folk: What do these feelings have to do with our life with God? Does feeling depressed separate us from God? Do people on the spiritual journey ever get angry or feel ashamed? Do we follow a God of desire or a God of control? Sorting out these questions helps us shape a spirituality of the negative emotions faithful both to our religious heritage and to our experience today.

Emotions Are Our Allies

Bad feelings make us miserable, but they often come bearing gifts. A negative emotion's gift sometimes comes in the self-examination it provokes. Emotional distress challenges familiar patterns—"something is not right!" Our regular ways of thinking and acting no longer work. Troubled and confused, we review our expectations, reexamine our values, raise questions about how our life is going. Our reflection carries the seeds of significant transformation; both personal and social change start here.

Frequently negative emotions benefit us by compelling us to act. "I feel so bad, I just have to do something about it." Sometimes what we do makes things worse, so good judgment and tact are crucial. But by giving us energy to follow through on effective behavior, negative emotions can help make things better.

Sometimes negative feelings' chief benefit is to apprentice us to mystery. Our emotions regularly remind us that life escapes our earnest control. And our feelings, especially those which bring pain, open us to deeper receptivity. Wrestling with our fear or anger, confounded by our shame and guilt, we savor a deeper awareness: "There is more here than meets the eye." A more profound appreciation of life's mystery invites greater acceptance of ourselves and other people, encouraging us to let go of some of our own insistent demands and welcome life as it is. Our feelings help us be at home in the world, wooing us, in the words of poet T.S. Eliot, "to sit still . . . even among these rocks."

In the chapters ahead we examine in closer detail the contributions that anger, guilt, shame, and depression make to our life and well-being. The chart here offers a preview of the benefits of the negative emotions when we welcome them as allies.

These benefits of the negative emotions are realized only with much discipline and many false starts. Each of these feelings easily escalates into a destructive sentiment. Unchecked, anger blossoms as rage and a thirst for revenge. Guilt mushrooms into obsessive self-punishment. Our healthy sense of shame succumbs to a crippling hesitance in social life. Depression, unattended, degenerates into a self-absorbed lethargy. Shaping these unruly sentiments into accomplices of our psychological and spiritual growth requires determined effort. The conviction that our negative emotions may come as gift instead of affliction, sources of grace rather than disgrace, guides this book. When we can decipher their code, our feelings reveal us to ourselves. They become allies on the perilous adventure of our adult lives.

Culture's Case Against Emotions

Human emotions are "probably always an illness of mind because both emotion and passion exclude the sovereignty of reason . . . emotion makes one more or less blind." This judgment of the eighteenth century philosopher Emmanuel Kant survives today in two cultural biases: emotions seen as *private passions* and as *irrational impulses*.

Benefits of the Negative Emotions

Anger   challenges us to right a wrong; calls us to
decisive action to protect from harm
something that we judge to be of genuine
value;

it leads to action in pursuit of *justice*.

Shame   affirms the necessary boundaries that support
our sense of self; warns of the risks of
premature exposure; protects the privacy
that makes genuine intimacy possible;

it is one of the roots of *personal dignity*.

Guilt   reminds us of the shape of our best self;
alerts us to discrepancies between ideals and
behavior; defends the commitments and
value-choices through which we give
meaning to our life;

it supports our sense of *personal integrity*.

Depression alerts us that something has become
intolerable; ordinary (rather than clinical)
depression invites us to re-examine our life;
its misery motivates us to face a challenge or
loss we have been avoiding;

it can ready us for *mature grieving* and
change.

Are Our Emotions Private?

Feelings seem uniquely our own. Guilt and shame are our most private
of possessions; anger and depression happen "inside my own skin."
America's cultural commitment to individualism feeds the temptation
to see our emotions as private events. Weighed down by our bad moods
we retreat further, warning even our closest friends to "just leave me

alone." Convinced other people just won't understand we retreat even further, searching out private remedies for private pain.

But emotions are more than private passions. In this book we explore an alternate perspective—emotions as social realities. As we shall see in chapter 3 and elsewhere, the rules that govern our feelings are primarily social in origin; the behaviors that express our emotions have a social function. Our feelings do not exist for us alone: emotions are social strategies directed toward our interaction with other people. Feelings attune us to the web of connections that links us to one another. "Emotions," as Willard Gaylin reminds us, "are not just directives to ourselves, but directives from others to us, indicating that we have been seen; that we have been understood; that we have been appreciated; that we have made contact."

And our feelings also alert us to troubles in our social world. Even depression, that most interior of sufferings, is often the body's way of warning us about an intolerable environment. When a social structure begins to crumble, its demise registers in the unrest, depression, and grief of the body politic. Sometimes negative emotions announce interior troubles, but often personal distress alerts us to danger in our social life. As theologian Beverly Wildung Harrison insists, "when we cannot feel, literally, we lose our connection to the world."

Do Our Passions Leave Us Passive?

Not only private, our emotions render us passive—so conventional wisdom tells us. Language and literature are filled with references to emotions as "passions" in the etymological sense: they *happen to* us. A person is *overcome* by guilt, *consumed* by anger, *paralyzed* by fear. Each verb is passive, suggesting our surrender in the face of forceful feelings. "I can't help it!" we plead. Indeed, considering ourselves victims of our emotions is consoling. If feelings are beyond our control, they are beyond our responsibility. In this understanding of emotional life, we don't have our feelings; they have us.

Social scientists and philosophers today pursue an alternate perspective. Philosopher Robert Solomon is a leading proponent of the view that we actively interpret and shape our emotions. In *The Passions*, Solomon urges us to recognize "emotions as our own *judgments*, with which we structure the world to our own purposes." When we make judgments about what we are feeling, we are not merely recording objective physiological stirrings; we are making sense of our world.

John Cheever notes in his *Journals* that "we perform our passions." Emotions are more than automatic reactions that we undergo. We are agents in our emotional life, not simply victims. When we identify our feelings, when we decide how to respond, we perform our passions. This familiar example may help.

> As Richard slowed at the intersection his pulse began to race. Traffic was already backed up at the four-way stop. One car would crawl through the intersection as the others waited like sheep. Then another would creep through a left turn. This was going to take all day! He cursed his misfortune, then began cursing the other drivers. "Where does all this traffic come from?" he steamed. "Why must these inexperienced drivers show up just when I am trying to get home? Will they never learn to deal effectively with something as simple as a four-way stop? It seems like the city's traffic system is designed to ruin my day."
>
> For years Richard would become enraged at this same intersection. But this day, as he waited impatiently for a hesitant driver to clear in front of him, Richard was struck with a new awareness. "I had always assumed that other drivers were the cause of my anger," he reported to friends later. "It wasn't my fault they didn't know how to drive, that they were blocking my way home. Very gradually the light dawned: when I arrived at the corner, the road was empty of any emotion. Then I flooded the intersection with my anger. Suddenly the street was awash with the irritation and upset that I brought to it. I was not the victim of this emotion, but its perpetrator."

Are Emotions Irrational?

Traditional theories have made thinking and feeling adversaries. A body/mind dualism casts reason in the role of a cool, detached master of our unruly passions. But the vision of reason and emotion as natural enemies no longer fits the evidence. Willard Gaylin voices a conviction widely shared among social scientists engaged in the study of human emotions: "Feelings are the instruments of rationality, not—as some would have it—alternatives to it." Emotions, he continues, "are fine tunings directing the ways in which we will meet and manipulate our environment."

Roberto Unger expands the discussion of emotion's particular contribution. Although passion has often been judged "the rebellious serf of reason," our emotions enjoy a kinship with our deepest desires that reason will never understand. "Reason gives us knowledge of the world," Unger comments, but "it cannot tell us in the final instance *what to want* or *what to do.*" Indispensable to the human journey, reason guides us as we analyze and clarify our experience. But reason alone does not rouse us to courageous or risky endeavors. Reason cannot ignite desire.

Likewise, reason "cannot provide the quality of sustained commitment that we need to pursue our most reasonable goals." Commitment springs from a source more visceral than cool cognition. Our dogged persistence in promises pledged is rooted in something deeper than rational plans and clear objectives. By tapping our desire, emotion sustains our commitment through dark days and dry seasons.

And "there are some revelations into our own and other people's humanity that we achieve only through experiences of passion." Empathy is a striking example of a passion that gives us a privileged glimpse into another's pain. This is a revelation that reason alone cannot muster. Our negative emotions, too, provide revelations. Guilt illumines personal failings of which we would prefer to remain ignorant. Anger reminds us of cherished values for which we are willing to fight. And grief coaxes us toward a life on the other side of a painful loss.

Our feelings alert us to our desires; they sustain us in our commitments; they give us glimpses of who we might be. For Unger the evidence of our lives shows "intimations of a richer interdependence between insight and impulse," confirming the links between passion and reason.

The A–I–M of the Emotions

Our friend and colleague James Zullo notes that every emotion involves arousal, interpretation, and movement. Examining these three elements helps us track the critical components of emotional life.

Arousal points to what happens in our bodies. Feelings have their root in physiology. Bodily changes trigger and accompany emotions: hormones are released; muscles expand or contract; shifts in blood flow affect oxygen supply to the brain. But the meaning of these physiological triggers remains notoriously vague. When my pulse speeds, am I indignant or afraid? Does this nervous stomach signal sadness or guilt? As my face flushes, am I feeling embarrassment or outrage?

Some few physiological arousals do appear solidly "wired" to certain emotions: feeling ashamed, the almost universal human response is to look down. But most arousals are at the same time emphatic and ambiguous. Typically, we notice our shortness of breath or an ache across the shoulders but are not yet sure what these stirrings signal. But by identifying a feeling—announcing "I'm afraid" or "I feel sad"—we make sense of a physical response. To know what we are feeling we have to give our arousal a name.

Emotions, then, involve *interpretation*. Not until we determine what our arousal *means* do we know what we are feeling. This example may help.

> Lillian shared a big meal with a colleague on her way home from work. Arriving home, she collected her messages from the telephone recorder. The third message brought news Lillian had been expecting, but dreading all the same. Her dear friend Anna called to announce her departure date. Over the past two months Anna had been weighing the decision to take a job in a distant city. The two friends spent many hours together discussing the pros and cons of the move. The new position was a definite career advance for Anna, one in which she was confident she would succeed. The biggest deficit in taking the job was its location. Anna, who was born and raised here, would have to move clear across the country. When Anna signed the contract, Lillian was genuinely happy for her. Over the three weeks since then, they had spent lots of time together working out the practical details of Anna's move. Hearing her friend's voice on the recorder lifted Lillian's spirits, but soon her good feelings were replaced by a more somber stirring.
>
> To avoid this still-shadowy distress, Lillian set about straightening up the apartment. Collecting the clothes for the laundry, dusting the book shelves, she tried to turn aside a growing heaviness of heart. Sitting for a moment to rest, she felt her distress expand. Trying to hold it off, she occupied herself with the details of tomorrow's work schedule. But soon the feeling returned. Lillian drifted into the kitchen. Opening the refrigerator, she surveyed its contents. "I'm a little hungry; I think I'll have a bite to eat."

Most of us have played out such a scene. A disturbing feeling comes as a nameless malaise. At first we try to ignore it. When our vague distress doesn't go away, we name it hunger—a discomfort we know how to remedy. The fact that we've just eaten is irrelevant. Only after many trips to the refrigerator do we realize we have misnamed our distress. The loneliness and sorrow Lillian felt at the news of her friend's imminent departure will not find remedy in food. A very different kind of nourishment is needed.

Lillian's experience shows how social contexts and personal moods shape our interpretations. These interpretations are how we *make sense* of our mute physiological stirrings and create our emotional world.

Emotions stir us first as physiological arousals, then elicit an interpretation of their meaning, and then impel us to act. Emotions are feelings that move us: they generate *movement*. Delighted, we dance for joy. Grateful, we write a warm note of thanks. Distressed by guilt, we call a friend to apologize. Emotion's arousal issues an alert, preparing us to act. Primed for "fight or flight," our body stands ready to rush toward the goal, to run from the danger, to repel the attack.

Sometimes dramatic action is called for: we dash into the burning building to save a child or fight to defend ourselves against a mugger's assault. More often, though, the appropriate response to emotional arousal is less clear and more complex. Should we challenge a colleague's racist remark now, or wait for a less public setting? Is a simple apology the best way to resolve a growing rift with my spouse, or should we commit ourselves to a lengthier look at the troublesome issues between us?

In the real world of social relationships, direct immediate action is not always useful or even possible. And what of those situations when better judgment warns that "doing nothing" is the right response? How do we deal with the intensity that lingers on? Physical activity often provides a release when we are caught in emotion's grip: going for a long walk or cleaning the house or working out at the gym. Sometimes relaxation helps: deep breathing exercises or therapeutic massage or the gentle luxury of a warm bath. Sometimes the best response is wonder, savoring the paradox of how strong and weak we find ourselves to be, how fragile is our hold on life—then letting go.

The interpretation that we give to a physiological arousal often tells us what to do. If we decide we are hungry rather than lonely, we move toward the refrigerator. The resolution of this bad feeling, we tell ourself, lies in food rather than companionship.

Sometimes the interpretation of what we are feeling is shaped by another judgment. If loneliness leaves the stoic in us feeling vulnerable, we will prefer to name this feeling hunger. If we have learned that anger is wrong or fear is a sign of weakness, denial will be our response when these arousals stir. "I'm just a bit tired," we murmur as we turn away from our feelings and try to get on with our life. Sometimes this strategy seems to work: our disappointment diminishes or the anger dissipates. But powerful feelings seldom simply disappear. Often they find other outlets. James Zullo succinctly describes the result of trying to bury our feelings in our body:

> We think about our feelings and get migraine headaches;
> We swallow our feelings and get ulcers;
> We carry the weight of our feelings and get back pain;
> We sit on our feelings and get hemorrhoids.

How We Hold Our Emotions

Christian life is about embraces—our experience of holding and being held. Faith begins in the embrace of a nurturing Creator; it expands in our companionship with Jesus Christ and the hold this person has on our life. Our fragile faith is tested and refined in a more disturbing embrace when—like Jacob in the Bible—we wrestle with a mysterious God who comes by night. Embraces build up the community of faith, where we hold some in affection and join with many in cooperation. As commitments mature, we hold each other accountable. And, unavoidably, there are times when we hold one another in the painful embrace of conflict.

But how do we hold our passions? Two opposing visions of spirituality contend to show us how. One spirituality counsels that emotions are unruly instincts erupting with blind and selfish force. The remedy is to hold these destructive emotions off—to hold them away and hold them still.

At the heart of this spirituality lurks the demon of dualism: The human person is split between body and soul, flesh and spirit. From this vision grew the conviction that holiness demands a distancing of the fragile spirit from the body's violent passions. The belief that we must hold off our emotions is fueled by the nightmares we see in the daily news: terrorist violence, domestic abuse, civil war. When we abandon ourselves to strong emotions we end by being held hostage to them. When we indulge our fear or wallow in regret, the journey of our life stalls.

The metaphor at the center of this spiritual tradition is *mastery*. Our unruly emotions are like wild animals that must be domesticated and controlled. The ideal of mastery powerfully attracted both stoicism and Christianity. In the centuries-long quest for control we have not always noticed how often mastery leads to denial. We seem to have our anger under control: we seldom shout, never hit other people, try to smile in adversity's face. Only later do we notice that anger, seemingly mastered, seldom disappears. Instead it goes underground, only to resurface in sarcasm and resentment. Not mastered after all, anger is just replaced by a more malignant mood.

A different spiritual tradition sees the negative emotions as ambiguous rather than destructive. Anger and fear and guilt are necessary disturbances, part of commitment's cost. These emotions are not irrational impulses, but arousals and alarms that carry clues to our best aspirations. Admittedly volatile and dangerous, our emotions remain potential partners in our search for holiness and health.

This more optimistic spirituality urges that we embrace our emotions with greater confidence. Rather than hold them off or hold them still, we yearn to embrace them in ways that tame and utilize their enormous energy. We cannot "master" our emotions because they are not our slaves. But we can learn to befriend these bewildering feelings. Befriending is a discipline that resists both the inclination to deny emotion and the temptation to abandon ourselves to it. Befriending begins in acknowledging what we feel, confident that our most frightening arousals are, finally, not our enemies.

At the heart of this spiritual tradition is the optimistic conviction that body and soul are not hopelessly alienated from one another. Emotion and reason remain open to a mutual influence. A partnership is possible between bodily impulse and spiritual insight. Here spirituality is not about avoiding the flesh and its blind demands, but about purifying and harmonizing our complex desires.

The *spirit* at the core of this spirituality is not a soul that is at odds with a hostile body or a spirit pining for release from the trials of the flesh. This spirit is the energy that springs from the breath-spirit (*ruach*) of the Jewish tradition and the vitality-spirit (*ch'i*) of the Chinese tradition. This spirit is the source of our liveliness and a link to our passionate Creator. Such spirit, so often wounded and scarred by our personal histories, is the energy in us that aspires to forge bonds of love and commitment and is willing to pay the price of guilt, loneliness, depression, and fear. In the following pages we will trace a spirituality that pursues befriending our emotions rather than mastery. Resonant with the wisdom of both East and West, this spirituality honors the disciplines required to transform our volatile emotions into reliable virtues.

Reflective Exercise

At the end of each chapter we offer readers the opportunity to trace their own understanding of the negative emotions. While the reflections are designed for personal use, their benefit is often greatly enhanced by sharing them with a friend or in a small group setting.

In this first reflective exercise, we ask you to revisit the past week or so of your life. In a quiet mood and place, recall the people you have been with, the work you were involved in, your predominant thoughts and moods. Then, make a list of the different feelings you experienced over the course of this period. Take your time with this listing. Now go back over your list and indicate which of these feelings you experienced as *negative*.

Finally, spend some time reflecting on these negative emotions: In your experience, why are these feelings *negative*? As you experienced these negative emotions, was there anything *positive* for you?

Additional Resources

Readers will find full publishing information for books and journal articles listed in the bibliography at the end of this book. Material drawn from newspapers is cited fully in the listings of Additional Resources.

A readable introduction to the concept of the negative emotions as positive resources is psychiatrist Willard Gaylin's *Feelings*; the quotations used in this chapter are drawn from his first chapter. Artist and writer Joan Erikson considers the interplay of sensual life and emotional development in *Wisdom of the Senses: The Way of Creativity*. We quote from p. 24 of Richard Bausch's novel *Rebel Powers*.

In *The Passions: The Myth and Nature of Human Emotion*, philosopher Robert Solomon makes a strong argument for the emotions as strategies of a responsible life; we quote p. xix of Introduction. Amélie Oksenberg Rorty has drawn together an impressive collection of essays from philosophers working on emotions in *Explaining Emotions*.

Psychologists today approach the study of emotions from many different perspectives. Of particular interest are *Emotion in Adult Development*, edited by Carol Zander Malatesta and Caroll E. Izard; *Nature's Mind* by Michael S. Gazzaniga; *Emotion and Adaptation* by Richard S. Lazarus; *The Biopsychology of Mood and Arousal* by Robert Thayer; "Facial Expression and Emotion" by Paul Ekman; and James Averill's playful and provocative discussion, "Six Metaphors of Emotion and Their Theoretical Extensions."

Social analyst Elizabeth Janeway explores the cognitive role of feelings in chapter 18 of *Powers of the Weak*. Roberto Unger offers an evocative vision of the contribution of passion to human life in *Passion: An Essay on Personality*; see pp. 101 and following for his observations quoted here. We are especially grateful to ethicist William Spohn for alerting us to Roberto Unger's exciting and challenging work; see Spohn's "Notes in Moral Theology: 1990," in *Theological Studies* (March 1991).

The comments on nurses' difficulty with emotions are found in "When Health Workers Stop to Mourn," *New York Times*, June 25, 1992. On the role of negative emotions in sexual addiction, see Ralph Earle and Gregory Crow's discussion in *Lonely All the Time*, pp. 101 and following. Howard Barbaree's research on rapists is reported by Daniel Goleman in the *New York Times*, December 10, 1991; see also Goleman's report, "Therapies Offer Hope for Sex Offenders," *New York Times*, April 14, 1992. Tina Adler reports Robert Pandino's research on young drug users in "Some Negative Feelings Can Fuel Abuse of Drugs," *American Psychological Association Monitor*, June 1990.

Mary Michael O'Shaughnessy offers a practical spirituality of emotional life in *Feelings and Emotions in Christian Living*; see also Frank McNulty's audiocassette series *A Theology of Feelings* and Clarence Thompson's audiocassette series *Healing the Emotions*. For an excellent overview of the role of God's creative breath (*ruach*), see Bernard Lee's *Jesus and the Metaphors of God*.

2

Befriending the Emotions

Language is the light of the emotions . . .
Paul Ricoeur

A painful feeling stirs in a dark corner of our heart. Hidden in the shadows, protected from the light of speech, a negative emotion exert its frightening force. We feel miserable. But is this misery fear or guilt or grief?

Words wrestle our feelings out of darkness, helping us befriend our emotional life. Befriending painful feelings doesn't magically take away the pain. But the effort of befriending opens us to a new relationship with our emotions: we no longer have to hold them off or hold them down or hold them still. And befriending points the way to the ordinary disciplines of emotional life—naming and taming.

Naming Our Emotions

Several years ago a friend of ours decided to fast once a week. Intrigued by this ancient practice, Douglas hoped fasting might help him think more clearly about his life. Busy at work during the first day of his new regime, he hardly noticed missing lunch. But by late afternoon the first sharp stab of hunger triggered panic: "I'm starving! I'll never make it through the rest of the day. I've got to have something to eat—now!" Startled by this rush of apprehension, Doug set aside his work for a moment to pay attention to what he was experiencing. For several minutes the panic prevailed, but then began to subside. Gradually Doug realized: this is what hunger feels like. Without food for nearly a day, his body complained. But Doug knew he was not about to perish.

His panic over starvation and survival, wired into our species from millennia past, turned out to be a false alarm. As the panic subsided, the arousal of hunger remained but its distress was only that: hunger. Once his distress had a name, the discomfort of being hungry was much more tolerable.

Naming our feelings is sometimes more traumatic. Pain suffered when we are children is often too threatening to be acknowledged and resolved. To survive the distress, we bury our agony in the dark cave of forgetfulness. From this subterranean hiding place, anonymous emotions continue to trouble us even when we have left childhood behind. Like a low-grade fever, some underlying sadness or shame spawns a discomfort that remains difficult to diagnose. But sometimes we break out of this amnesia. Growing stronger and more resilient in adult life readies us to revisit the dark corners of our heart. Parts of our past that had been excluded from memory come to light.

Poet Joe Kogel describes such a memory. Recalling a family fight in which his mother had fallen down a flight of stairs, he begins to remember the truth about his past and the origins of his nameless pain.

> I could not have known then
> That I would learn to love this memory,
> Rub it smooth between my fingers,
> A velvety stone found on a beautiful beach.
> I hold this stone like a charm.

> The charm is not the pain.
> But when I give myself back my pain,
> I make myself real
> And when I am real, I'm lucky.
> I am lucky knowing it was wrong and a lie.
> What we called a happy family was not.
> I . . . hid in small rooms. Until now.

Decades of vague unhappiness suddenly find their focus in remembered pain. The poet embraces this long forgotten injury not as an exercise in masochism or self-absorption nor simply as an opportunity to blame. "The charm is not the pain." The pain has no value in itself. Its charm is its power, when remembered, to reconnect him with himself. Healing begins "when I give myself back my pain." Naming the pain—"what we called a happy family was not"—rescues his past from oblivion. The pretense of a happy family and the distortions demanded to protect this illusion fall away. "I make myself real."

Finding the Correct Name

Naming our emotions gives us clues for how to respond to them. A colleague's story shows how this is so.

> Several years ago Janet left a faculty position at a college located in a rural community, to begin working as an education consultant. Traveling frequently, she soon became aware of a troubling feeling that accompanied her on most of these trips. Boarding the small commuter plane that would bring her to the major airport hub nearby, Janet became increasingly irritated. In her words, "I'd start by feeling annoyed by the shuffle of noisy passengers making their way down the narrow aisle. Other people's hand luggage bumping my arm and their inane conversation as they settled in their seats heightened my agitation. At first I misnamed this arousal as anger. I'd blame the people around me who made the departure uncomfortable. Inwardly I fumed and fussed, rehearsing stinging comments to settle them in their seats quietly. All this "inner talk" only increased my furor.
>
> "Over several months I realized gradually that I was not angry but anxious. Suddenly my unsettled feeling was easier to understand: I was leaving home with its familiar and safe surroundings; I would be confined for a time in an enclosed public space; I was traveling to an unfamiliar location to give a seminar to an unknown group of people, where my professional reputation would be on the line. No wonder I was not completely at ease; what I was feeling was fear!
>
> "Once I found the correct name for my arousal, the experience changed significantly. My fellow-travelers were no longer culprits to be subdued or punished. And having found the right name, I knew better how to respond. Now when I board a plane, instead of preparing caustic but useless remarks to control the other passengers' behavior, I begin deep-breathing exercises. The force of this natural tranquillizer calms my mind and lessens the anxiety I feel. Now traveling is much easier for me."

This everyday example of finding the right name for an emotion is reinforced by recent research on panic attacks. People subject to these assaults share distressing symptoms: sharp chest pains occur, accompanied by profuse sweating; they report feeling dizzy and a sense of impending doom. These frightening signals convince many sufferers they are having a heart attack. After frequent trips to the emergency room and regular physical examinations reveal no evidence of heart trouble, patients and physicians have come to recognize these symptoms as signs not of heart attack but of panic disorder. Equipped with the correct name for their distress, people know what to do when these attacks arise. In cognitive-behavior therapy sessions they learn to identify the earliest signs of panic arousal and to respond with breathing exercises. Staying with this discipline yields compelling results. As one panic survivor remarked, "Then the anxiety subsides and you realize it's just a wave of anxiety, not a heart attack." The ability to manage their distress begins in finding the right name for what they are feeling.

Naming the Deep Theme

Even knowing the name of an emotion that troubles us may not immediately reveal its source. We feel guilty, but why? Or certain situations enrage us for no apparent reason. Often the effort to name a mysterious feeling uncovers deeper themes. Recall Richard, whom we met in chapter 1.

> Regularly infuriated in heavy traffic, Richard accurately named his arousal anger. Right away he identified the obvious circumstances that contributed to his irritation—living in a heavily populated area, having to commute long-distances regularly for his work, holding himself to the demands of a busy schedule. Yet having anger's name didn't do much to help him moderate its negative force. Attending a workshop session several months later, Richard discovered another provocation at play when he was behind the wheel. The workshop leader introduced an imaginative exercise, instructing Richard to fantasize the best possible experience of driving in traffic. A sudden vision came to him: a world in which all the traffic lights are green! In the fantasy, synchronized switches turned each traffic light green as Richard approached the intersection. The fantasy expanded: as Richard moved through life, all roads opened up before him; traffic halts, crowds part, as he moves forward unimpeded and in control.
>
> Exploring this fantasy, Richard recognized the childish response

still triggered in him by every stoplight: "this restraint should not happen to me! I should never have to be bothered by other people!" When this underlying theme emerged with such embarrassing clarity, Richard broke into laughter. The next time he felt anger surge as he approached a traffic light, Richard said aloud with great seriousness: "I should never have to wait!" At the sound of this outrageous demand, he laughed again and felt the anger dissolve. Identifying and exposing this hidden theme gave Richard insight into his anger and a perspective on how to change his behavior.

Noting his improved civility behind the wheel, Richard's wife presented him with a bumper sticker carrying the slogan "Be a Buddha of the Road." This has become a family mantra: confronting snarled traffic, inevitable car-pool delays, or the frequent inconvenience of road repairs, family members encourage each other with the chant, "Be a buddha of the road."

When a perplexing emotion gives up some of its hold over us, we know we have found its name. Naming rescues our emotions from the recesses of our heart and readies us to embrace their power in our life.

Taming the Negative Emotions

Negative emotions carry both feelings of pain and the impulse to act. The painful feelings grab our attention first. If we focus only on the pain, we risk losing sight of the gift of the emotion—its energy for change.

Releasing this gift requires taming our negative emotions. To start, we must see the pain for what it is—a bad feeling about something good. Pain is an alarm, a signpost, a signal for our survival. Our distress points beyond itself.

Psychologist Willard Gaylin offers a useful analogy: A negative emotion is like a fever—a painful experience that has a positive purpose. The fever gets our attention; it signals something is wrong, often before we are otherwise aware of the problem. Sometimes training our healing efforts on the fever itself is important. We try to bring the patient's temperature down, especially if it is sufficiently high to be life-threatening. We want to make the sick person as comfortable as possible, so that the body's own resources may be brought to bear on the healing. But we recognize that to focus our efforts just on the fever is to miss the point.

A fever is a symptom of another, more serious distress. The high temperature indicates that the body is mobilizing its resources to attack an infection or repulse an intruding agent. So we turn our attention to tracking this deeper cause, wanting to direct our healing efforts at the source rather than the symptom. If we let the fever distract us from this more complicated process of accurate diagnosis and proper treatment, we may alleviate the pain in the short run but our intervention may not be of any long-range help. In fact, the patient may get worse.

Like a fever, a painful emotion is an alarm, a signpost, a signal for our survival. The pain gets our attention, but the distress points beyond itself—alerting us to information we might otherwise miss, signaling something significant that we might otherwise take for granted.

Respecting pain as a signal starts the taming process. But often our painful feelings serve less as a signal than as a stop sign. Emotional distress debilitates us, bringing our life to a halt. Confronted by negative emotions, then, many of us respond by trying to get rid of the pain. The problem with this approach is that it seldom really works. Instead further isolation results: to avoid painful feelings we silence our inner voice and cut ourselves off from any experience or relationship that seems threatening.

Taming our negative emotions demands developing personal strategies to help us honor our pain, without simply succumbing to it. Discovering what calms us under stress is a good place to start. Going for a swim or watching a sunset, seeking strenuous exercise or a relaxing massage, quieting ourselves in the receptive stance of meditation or prayer: in each of these strategies we learn to calm our distress long enough to discern its meaning.

But concentrating too intently on our emotional distress is risky. The first risk is that we will begin to wallow in the pain. Giving too much attention to our turmoil overshadows the potential gifts of the negative emotion—greater insight into our life and renewed energy to make things different. We let our pain drag us down toward helplessness rather than empowering us for action.

A focus on getting rid of our pain also makes us vulnerable to the "quick fix." Turning to drugs—prescription or illegal—to deaden the distress, we again short circuit the emotion's energy. No learning occurs, no effective action results.

To concentrate on eliminating painful feelings raises another risk—

avoidance becomes our chief strategy. Sometimes avoidance works. Steering clear of situations that make us afraid, of people who shame us, of memories that reawaken our rage often makes sense. But as a regular response, avoidance exacts a toll. To avoid fear we settle for a lifestyle that includes no risks. To avoid anger we consistently turn back from asserting our opinions or our needs. To avoid guilt we build defenses of denial, protecting ourselves from self-scrutiny. To avoid shame we retreat from any closeness with others that might leave us exposed—our ideas, our hopes, our true self. In each case, efforts to avoid negative emotions diminish our life. For most of us, this empty calm comes at too high a price.

Painful emotion comes in part as ally, provoking reflection and challenging us to act. So befriending the negative emotions rarely means avoiding the pain. Instead, taming enables us to embrace the emotion—long enough to discern its message, long enough to evaluate its import, long enough to use its energy to fuel the action required. Taming doesn't imply domesticating our feelings, rendering them docile, housebroken, and spayed. Taming provokes positive change, focusing emotional energy into actions that can help us.

Taming begins in acknowledging what we are feeling. Its discipline leads us between the extremes of denying an emotion ("I am *not* angry!") and succumbing to it. Here, as in the classic understanding, virtue lies in the middle: between *refusing* to feel anything and *abandoning* ourselves to emotion's immediate demands. This virtuous response takes many forms. We tame anger by learning to channel its force into fruitful confrontation. We tame the arousal of petulant rage or false guilt by developing techniques that dissipate their energy. Throughout, taming resists the temptation to cling to the feelings that bring us down.

Harboring Emotion

Taming warns us not to harbor negative feelings. The metaphor of *harboring* suggests an inlet—our heart—into which a feeling of loneliness or self-pity or jealousy floats, looking for a place to reside. A participant of one of our courses tells this story on herself.

> I was on the way outside to work in my garden when the mail arrived. One letter held an invitation to write a review of an about-

to-be-published book, a collection of essays on marriage. Glancing through the letter as I walked toward the garden, at first I felt flattered. But as I began to pull weeds along the edge of the garden I noticed that "feeling flattered" had suddenly been replaced by another emotion. "Why hadn't the editors of the book asked me to contribute a chapter?" I wondered. "I know more on the topic of marriage than many of these other people!" Now, instead of being flattered, I felt offended. I was upset and—hating to admit it—envious of the writers whose work was showcased in the book. I turned back to my weeding, but before long this sour feeling returned. Envy seemed to be asking for safe harbor, a place to drop anchor for a longer stay. My wounded honor wanted permission to pout. Again I dismissed the envy and turned back to the weeds. Ten minutes later, the emotion reappeared, bobbing up and down at the edge of my harbor, asking again for attention. This time I decided to spend a few moments acknowledging my disappointment and nursing my wounded pride. Then, wishing them well, I sent these visitors on their way. No room in my harbor today. After a few minutes, the gentle rhythm of pulling weeds restored my sense of peace.

Harboring indulges the negative emotions, expanding their claims and absorbing our attention. The metaphor of harboring helps us recognize our own complicity in feeling bad. A young adult friend gives an example. Chris frequently feels lonely, an emotion he dreads. But as he now recognizes, Chris often gives himself over to the feelings. "When I feel a mood of loneliness descending, I'll usually try to stay off by myself. I'll play romantically sad music; I'll turn off the phone so that no one can reach me. It's like I don't want to be distracted from my melancholy!"

Crossing the Bridge

Harboring an emotion, we cling to it. Instead of seizing its energy to face a challenge, we bog down. Rather than using the arousal to confront a threat, we mull it over. A harbored emotion becomes chronic, corroding our insides and spoiling our relationships with others. Author Thomas Buckley describes such a prolonged attachment to anger:

> The "sinfulness" of anger may not lie in anger itself but in prolonged attachment to it; in the refusal, out of fear, to let ourselves back

into the impermanent world of interrelationship, *across the bridge of sadness* [our emphasis].

When we cling to feelings of anger or loneliness or guilt, we refuse this crossing. We choose, instead, to dwell in a private world of regret and self-pity. In Buckley's words, this is a "refusal of grief, and thus of the possibility of going through and beyond both anger and sorrow." But what is this bridge of sadness and how are we to cross it?

The bridge is constructed by all the disciplines by which we *make something* of our painful emotions. On one side of the bridge is raw pain, the mute, nameless hurt we feel on the inside. Certain moods— sadness, guiltiness, loneliness—seem to envelop us, absorbing attention and deterring us from action. But emotions are transitive: they are meant to move us, to impel us to face a threat or to seek forgiveness—to cross the bridge.

In *The Road Less Traveled*, Scott Peck describes the transformation of pain into suffering. Pain is the blunt and often mute experience of misery. We feel terrible, without knowing why. Or we know why—a child has died or a marriage ended—but we can do nothing about it. Stunned by pain, we are struck dumb; we groan but are rendered speechless. We can remain stuck in this meaningless pain, swallowed alive by grief or guilt. Such pain tells us nothing, leads us nowhere. The only remedy seems to be medication to numb the hurt. Stranded on this side of the bridge, we register our pain in depression or sarcasm or self-contempt.

As we struggle to name our distress, we start to cross the bridge. Meaningless pain transforms into suffering. Here *suffering* does not signify passive acceptance; it does not indicate we relish our hurt or are willing to undergo more injury. Pain's transformation into suffering begins when we are willing, in John Bradshaw's words, "to feel as bad as we really feel."

Recent studies of nurses who served in Vietnam underscore the need to move pain into suffering. A unique feature of the war in Vietnam was the medical-evacuation helicopter. For the first time, severely wounded soldiers could be rapidly transported to medical units. Here nurses and doctors, struggling to mend hideous injuries, watched innumerable patients die in their hands. The combination of endless violence and the impotence of the medical personnel generated a profound rage and grief, in a setting where there was no opportunity to acknowledge these powerful emotions. The nurses often felt they were *not entitled* to express their feelings of anger and loss; only the front-line soldier had the right to such emotions.

When these nurses returned from duty in Vietnam they often plunged into hyperactive lives, or depression, or both. As increasing numbers of nurses sought therapy, the medical community recognized in them the symptoms of post-traumatic shock syndrome. Given the opportunity to acknowledge their negative feelings in counseling sessions and support groups, many nurses found their symptoms of frenetic activity and depression disappearing. The senseless pain of the war was being transformed and humanized into suffering.

William Stringfellow—a lawyer, theologian, and poet—gives another description of the journey across the bridge from pain to suffering. In "The Joy of Mourning," Stringfellow recalls his response to the death of Anthony, his life companion. At first, he is engulfed by grief, an emotion he understands "to be the total experience of loss, anger, outrage, fear, regret, melancholy, abandonment, temptation, bereftness, helplessness suffered privately, within one's self, in response to the happening of death." In case we have missed the point, he adds: "Grieving is about weeping and wailing and gnashing of teeth."

Stringfellow recognizes that regret and gratitude, anger and affection are all jumbled together in the initial shock of his friend's death. His own healing, and the ability to celebrate his companion's life, will require sorting out these emotions. For Stringfellow, this will mean the transformation of grief into mourning. "I comprehend mourning as the liturgies of recollection, memorial, affection, honor, gratitude, confession, empathy, intercession, meditation, anticipation for the life of the one who is dead." Again he adds: "Mourning is about rejoicing. . . . I enjoy mourning Anthony."

On one side of the bridge of sadness, stunning grief accumulates. Through rituals of memory and tears and thanksgiving, we can turn grief into mourning. Mourning is the *work* of grief. If we refuse the work of mourning, our grief will consume us. But when we mourn, we begin to transform pain into suffering—a sorrow that will enrich instead of cripple.

The final bridge we cross is our own death. Learning of our terminal illness floods us with emotions of anger, regret, and even bitterness. Why me? Why now? What are we to do with the pain and panic of our own death? In *Intoxicated by My Illness*, Anatole Broyard describes his efforts to become the main actor, rather than the mere victim of his own impending death. Broyard suggests that "illness is primarily a drama, and it should be possible to enjoy it as well as suffer it." To savor an illness, we have to give it voice. "I would advise every sick person to evolve a style or develop a voice for his or her illness." This effort to actively embrace our approaching death "is another way of meeting it on your own grounds, of making it a mere character in your narrative."

By writing of his coming death, Broyard attempts what all literature aspires to achieve: sufficiently distancing an experience so that we can embrace it again as our own. Broyard turns his death into a drama, writing a role for himself. Having gained this perspective on death, he can step into the role and play it with vigor.

Being an active participant in sickness, even in mortal illness, we hold our hurt in a way that escapes both depression and self-pity. In the words of Broyard's wife, "He did not conquer his cancer, but he triumphed in the way he lived and wrote about it."

Christians believe that the life and death of Jesus shows us how to cross the bridge of the negative emotions. The gospel calls us to take up our cross and follow Jesus. Too often in Christian history, naive piety transformed this challenge into an endorsement of victimhood. The "good Christian" must accept his poverty or her abusive spouse; the virtuous person should put up with all manner of discomfort and injustice. But the invocation to take up the cross does not counsel passivity. It acknowledges, instead, that painful crises come to each of us and that we can *do something* about these troubles. We can seize the pain and loss that come our way, and do with them what Jesus did. At the death of his friend Lazarus, Jesus was moved to tears and groans. Facing the end of his own life, he initially struggled, then finally embraced death without indignity or shame. Neither a stoic nor a victim, Jesus lived the delights and distress of his life to the full; he performed his passions. Following him, we struggle to find the way across our own bridge of sadness.

Befriending the negative emotions is a lifelong adventure. Very gradually we uncover the origins of these forceful and frightening sentiments. Armed with their names, we begin to tame them, to distinguish between their healthy and destructive potential. Gingerly, we familiarize ourselves with anger and shame and depression. When we harness the energy of anger to challenge a wrong, instead of drowning in our resentment, we cross the bridge. When we recognize the source of a depression and take actions to change these conditions, we cross the bridge. When we learn to hold our hurt before God in prayer, instead of harboring our grief, we cross the bridge.

But what holds us back? Buckley suggests it is "out of fear" and "the refusal of grief" that we cling to our negative emotions. Sometimes self-pity blocks the crossing; sometimes lack of support bogs us down. Refusing to risk this crossing mires us in lethal patterns. Harbored, anger or guilt or regret eventually ruin us. Perhaps it is to this hazard the gospel points in the warning not to so love our life that we lose it.

What helps us across the bridge of sadness? As social creatures, we rely on the encouragement of others. Friends and family members, mentors and pastoral ministers model how to tame our emotions of anger and guilt and shame. We rely, too, on the rituals that society and religious faith provide: ceremonies of grieving and reconciliation that face us in the right direction and pace us on the risky journey of letting go.

Finally, when we dare to cross the bridge, where do we arrive? In Buckley's words, we come into "the impermanent world of interrelationship." *Impermanent* is the crucial word here: we cross the bridge back into a world filled with loss and failure, a land scarred by sin and injury. We leave behind fantasies of perfectionism and of friendships that never change. If the world we reenter is impermanent, it is also inhabited by forgiveness. This is not a place of hatred or resentment, of bitterness or revenge. On this side of the bridge our negative emotions become our allies helping us face the dangers and reconciliations that mark our path.

Reflective Exercise

First, identify a feeling you have become more comfortable with recently. This may be a positive emotion such as joy or confidence or compassion, or a more problematic feeling such as jealousy or resentment or fear. Spend some time remembering what helped you befriend this emotion. Be as concrete as you can; give some examples.

Then identify a troublesome feeling that you are sometimes tempted to harbor. Use your imagination: picture this emotion swimming into your heart as if into a bay of water. How do you permit this emotion to drop anchor; what attitudes or behaviors or beliefs encourage the feeling to linger in your heart? Why do you harbor this feeling; what is its "perverse payoff" for you? Concretely, what action can you take to resist harboring this emotion in the future?

Additional Resources

Paul Ricoeur explores the role of language in *The Symbolism of Evil*: "Language is the light of the emotions. Through confession the consciousness of fault is brought into the light of speech; through confession man remains speech, even in the experience of his own absurdity, suffering and anguish" (p. 7). At the close of this profound book, Ricoeur explains that symbols "rescue feeling and even fear from silence and confusion; they provide a language for avowal, for confession; in virtue of them, man remains language through and through" (p. 350), and observes that "it is by *interpreting* that we can *hear* again" (p. 351).

Joe Kogel's poetic reflection on his own history appeared in *Los Angeles Times*, September 6, 1989. For a discussion of the tendency to confuse panic attacks with genuine heart attacks, see "Heart Seizure or Panic Attack? Disorder Is A Terrifying Mimic," *New York Times*, January 8, 1992. Laura Palmer discusses "The Nurses of Vietnam, Still Wounded" in the *New York Times Magazine*, November 7, 1993, pp. 36 and following.

In *Emotion* Jungian psychologist James Hillman offers a comprehensive overview of psychological theories of affective life; urging counselors to adopt a therapeutic approach closer to befriending than to dispelling emotion, Hillman notes that "emotions respond immediately to the truth of things. They are the most alert form of attention" (p. xii). Thomas Buckley examines anger's "sinfulness" in "The Seven Deadly Sins," *Parabola* (Winter 1985), p. 6. Scott Peck distinguishes pain from suffering in chapter 1 of *The Road Less Traveled*.

William Stringfellow charts his movement beyond grief in "The Joy of Mourning," *Sojourners* (April 1982), pp. 29–32. Anatole Broyard demonstrates his own assertive effort to name and tame his dying in *Intoxicated by My Illness*; we quote from pp. xviii, 7, and 61. Theologian John Carmody explores the spiritual dimensions of befriending negative experience in *How to Handle Trouble* and *Cancer and Faith: Reflections on Living with a Terminal Illness*.

3

Learning How to Feel

Life was hard in the hinterland . . .
          . . . where the mode
was stoic, and embarrassment stood in
    the way of affect:
a mother having been alarmingly seen
    in tears, once only
we brought her a fistful of johnny-
    jump-ups from the garden,
"because you were crying"—and saw
    we'd done the wrong thing.

Amy Clampitt

Human beings have no raw instincts, anthropologists insist. Our impulses always come "cooked," part of the cultural stew of expectations and prohibitions that prevail in each society. Our most private feelings are seasoned in this communal pot.

In our emotional lives, then, biology and culture embrace. Feelings like joy or guilt or regret are more than spontaneous reactions; they are social constructions. Emotions are learned responses, crafted on our culture's design. And in the school of the emotions, family is our first teacher. The children in Amy Clampitt's poem, seeing their mother's tears, presented flowers in hopes of consoling her. Then they "saw we'd done the wrong thing." Gradually, often painfully, we grasp emotion's rules.

From the start, our parents instruct us in what we are feeling. Before we are able to do this for ourselves, they name our arousals for us. Take a familiar example: a nightmare's terror awakens a child. Her cries bring mother rushing to her bedside. Holding her daughter close, mother rocks her gently as she soothes, "Did a bad dream frighten you, my baby? No wonder you're afraid! But everything's all right. Mommy's here; nothing will hurt you now." The little girl learns this terrible feeling has a name—fear. And she takes away more than vocabulary. Her parent's response also carries an evaluation. A warm embrace links this distressing feeling with care and protection; this emotion is less horrible now because a cry will bring someone who is stronger than the nightmare. But if the parent responds with a stern admonition— "Stop crying, you silly child. There's nothing to be afraid of here. Be a big girl and go back to sleep!"—the child learns another rule of her family's culture: fearful feelings are not acceptable here.

Naming our emotions for us, family members give us the words we will use to identify our own arousals. The vocabulary of feelings is not simply their own invention; these names pass on a particular culture's map of emotional life. Home life instructs us about managing feelings, too. Partly by their words, even more by their actions, our caregivers provide performance rules—how feelings are to be expressed, when they should be controlled, which must be denied. Later, school and neighborhood and church join the cultural chorus reinforcing the names and norms for what we are feeling.

The Social Construction of Emotions

We are born biologically unfinished. Unlike salmon or spiders, bison or bees, our instincts are indeterminate—wonderfully flexible and dangerously unformed. The vocation of human culture is to shape surges of feeling and desire into socially useful emotions. Without this formation, as anthropologist Clifford Geertz cautions, we would be left "a kind of formless monster with neither sense of direction nor power of self-control, a chaos of spasmodic impulse and vague emotions."

Emotions then are social strategies, personal actions that follow a communal script. As each of us learns to speak in the shared vocabulary of our culture's language, so we learn to feel within the shared categories of our culture's emotional range. In *Vanquished Nation, Broken Spirit* the eminent historian Jacob Neusner describes the social strategy developed within Jewish culture to deal with the negative emotions. After the Romans destroyed Jerusalem in the year 70, the Jews were a defeated people. In this dangerous climate of political subjugation, their survival was at risk. Acutely aware that any public display of anger or arrogance could provoke retaliation on the whole group, the Jewish community responded by crafting an approved repertoire of feelings. "The natural traits of humanity: anger, rebellion, arrogance, selfishness" had to be suppressed, replaced by what Neusner poignantly describes as the "virtues of the broken heart."

The emotion of anger became a *kosher emotion*. "When we realize that *kosher* emotions compare to *kosher* foods, we penetrate the heart of matters. The sages do not prohibit *wanting* to eat pork, they prohibit eating it." For a subject people, an emotion such as anger became especially dangerous: Jews could feel outrage, but they must not express it. When a culture forbids the direct expression of anger, some compensatory response is likely; *chutzpa* may be the emotional balance that Jewish culture provided for its proscription of public anger.

In his book *Latinos*, Earl Shorris describes a comparable cultural response, shaping the emotions of an oppressed community. After the Spanish conquest, the inhabitants of South and Central America became subject peoples. To survive oppression and hardship, these cultures developed the emotional response of *aguantar*: "patient endurance." Mexicans and other Latin Americans became recognized for their ability to suffer—and survive—poverty and mistreatment. This social emotion was especially apt for subject cultures; in a blend of stoicism and courage, members learned to endure their fate bravely. But, as Shorris and others have observed, such patient endurance can degenerate from a virtue (a strategy of personal and group survival) to a liability (a habituation to past patterns of oppression). "*Aguantar* does not mean surrender; it is not a bargain. The one who endures does not do so gladly; sullenness lives under the surface; the bowed head hides the rage of despair"—a rage likely to find its release in domestic violence. Thus, through the social construction of emotions, cultures both help us survive and bind us to particular social arrangements.

The Social Emotion of Boredom

The corrosive mood of boredom furnishes a clear example of how cultural forces generate personal feeling. Living in poverty, caught in a dull job, stranded in a stagnated marriage, we are likely to experience this debilitating emotion. Roberto Unger provides a compelling definition: "Boredom is, in fact, the weight of unused capacity, an intimation of the freedom from which the self has hidden."

Unger's analysis begins in our *capacity*: the potential and promise that energize the human person. When this capacity is blocked or defeated, fallow energy begins to press upon us—"the weight of unused capacity." A mood of boredom signals the growing suspicion that there is nothing worth doing. Whether we are surrounded by the despair of the inner city or the superficialities of suburban life, we feel energy drain away as we face barren days and duties without merit.

This stifling mood is more than a bad feeling. Boredom functions as an alert, protesting our diminishment. Its monotony carries "an intimation of the freedom from which the self has hidden." Our ennui announces we have disengaged; the very announcement forces us to recognize our complicity.

A social emotion, boredom both arises from our environment and provokes culture to provide a cure. Every culture has a calling to engage the energies of its people, to channel each individual's capacity in productive and creative directions. By offering challenging goals, stimulating workplaces, and multiple options for public service, a society opens ways for its members to contribute to the common good. But societies are tempted to simply drain off the untapped energy of its citizens by providing them with diversions—whether the bread and circuses of the Roman empire in decline or the home shopping channels of cable television. Unger describes the unhealthy dynamic of this organized distraction as "the search for novelty without peril . . . a temporary release from routine."

Many cultural activities refresh us and ready us for another day of work. Some even ascend to art, stirring in us the cleansing catharsis that opens us to change and renewal. But these temporary distractions often function as mere escapes, as "diversions" in Unger's vocabulary. Watching endless television soap operas or spending our evenings at the local bar risks diverting our attention for a short time without lifting "the weight of unused capacity" that still afflicts us. By providing too many distractions that never challenge and too many diversions that fail to refresh, a culture fails its citizens.

Unger describes this cycle of diversion and dull routine, so apparent in American life today:

> The failed life is the life that alternates between the stagnation of routinized conduct and vision and the restless craving for momentary release.

A consumer society promises momentary release from boredom in shopping or sports or self-indulgence, but these provide mock deliverance. Waiting for us at home or the workplace is the crushing weight of our unused capacity. Caught up in a culture's tedium, we often blame ourself. But boredom is a social disease, a cultural strategy of social control.

Cultural Metaphors of Guilt

Tracing the influence of culture on our feelings brings us soon to shame and guilt. These essentially social emotions monitor our belonging, alerting us when we fail to fit in. We *learn* to feel guilty, as parents and other authorities instruct us when and why to experience this painful emotion. The rules of guilt they teach have roots in cultural and religious traditions. In Western societies, two biblical images have powerfully shaped the cultural vision of guilt.

The inhabitants of ancient Israel understood their religious failures as breaking the covenant with God. Our religious ancestors saw their life as a web of social relationships—in the family, among the different clans, with Yahweh. Within this sustaining network, they survived and thrived as a people. Outside this vital web—in the hostile desert or among alien tribes—life was in jeopardy. Thus to injure this network of belonging was to threaten death and deserve punishment. The meaning of life was knit together in the bonds that connected them as members of this believing community. The purpose of this people was summed up in their covenant with Yahweh; fidelity to this relationship meant life and blessings. To undermine or compromise these networks of life was to become guilty of sin.

A very different metaphor of failure appears in the Christian gospel. The New Testament word for sin, *hamartia*, means "to miss the mark." Calling to mind the picture of an archer aiming at a distant target, this image likens moral behavior to achieving a goal. In this metaphor, life is portrayed as the pursuit of an objective ideal more than as fidelity to a web of relationships.

"Honoring the covenant" focuses on belonging; "missing the mark" emphasizes achievement. Together these images have shaped Western culture's experience of guilt. The metaphor of covenant speaks especially to those who place high value on relationships. Women, for example, are typically socialized to a strong sense of responsibility for establishing and maintaining the social connections of family and friendship. Understandably, then, many women feel guilt most keenly over injuries to their social network. Many men have been socialized to pursue personal achievement more than relationships. For men like this, "hitting the mark" expresses the sense of responsibility. Holding themselves accountable to performance goals, judging themselves according to external standards of success, these men feel guilt most keenly when they sense they have "missed the mark."

Purifying the Metaphors of Guilt

At their best these two metaphors of guilt are complementary. Every adult belongs to social networks; each of us seeks personal goals. So caring for our relationships and struggling to achieve our ideals are concerns shared by us all, not tasks limited to one gender or the other. And acknowledging the truth of *both* these images often helps heal guilt's destructive force in our lives. Some women, holding themselves responsible for making relationships go well, have considerable trouble with guilt. The web of family and friendship is a complex arrangement. Troubles anywhere in the extended network vibrate across the web. Defining boundaries of personal responsibility is not easy: "How can I ease the tension between my husband and our oldest son? Am I to blame for the failure of my daughter's marriage? Where does my responsibility for my aging parents leave off?" A woman, sensitive to the dynamics of relationships, often translates this sensitivity into obligation: "I have to fix it." If she cannot make things better, she very likely feels guilty: "I have failed the relationship."

We purify the metaphor of guilt as "breaking the covenant" when we recognize that not all covenants are holy. Sometimes we enter into contracts that are unhealthy.

> I must have decided somewhere along the way to be unfailingly friendly and never offend anyone. But being faithful to this unrealistic demand—this covenant I have made with myself—has crippled my ability to face conflict and to speak out against the injustices I see. For me to mature, this covenant has to be broken. I know I'll experience pangs of guilt when I raise my voice or disagree with other people, but I must do it anyway.

The metaphor of missing the mark allows for a more focused sense of responsibility and, thus, of guilt. In this image we leave home— and its web of responsibilities—to go to the archery range. This setting itself encourages us to set clear boundaries: the archer aims at a single identified target, ignoring other goals. And the athletic metaphor moderates our guilt another way, since the world of sport teaches us to incorporate failure into the game. Not every arrow hits the bull's-eye, even for the champion archer. A baseball player who achieves a .300 batting average is considered a success, yet this is a person who fails 70 percent of the time. A basketball player who makes just 55 percent of her shots is considered a star player. Playing sports can teach us to learn from our mistakes rather than to blame or punish ourselves for them. Tennis champion Billie Jean King reframes the painful experience of failing: "For me, losing a tennis match isn't failure, it's research."

The metaphor of hitting the mark also awaits purification. Early on we inherit high ideals of achievement: to be as good in school as our sister; to earn more money than our father; to become the doctor our parents have always wanted. Only later does the realization dawn, "these goals were placed on my archery range before I arrived with my bow and arrow. For years I have been shooting at somebody else's target!"

Christianity and the Negative Emotions

Christianity's influence on our emotions goes far beyond these metaphors of guilt. From our origins, Christians have harbored deep suspicions about the world of feeling. As early as the second century two voices—one secular and one Christian—spoke out eloquently against passion, profoundly influencing our religious heritage. Marcus Aurelius, Roman emperor and stoic philosopher, mused in his journal about "the puppet strings of passion." We identify easily with this image: an instant anger provokes us into injuring a friend; a spasm of fear collapses our resolve; a sudden sexual arousal blinds us to commitments already pledged.

The stoic ideal of Marcus Aurelius was serenity, a dispassionate detachment that would rescue an individual from the maelstrom of emotions. By mastering our moods, he was convinced, we could find peace and equanimity. "It now lies within my power that there be no vice or passion, *no disturbance at all*, in this my soul, but I see all things for what they are and deal with them on their merits" [emphasis added].

The emotion of grief overwhelms us only if we forget that loss and death are part of life's natural rhythm. "Do not be entirely swept along by the thought of another's grief. Help him as far as you can . . . do not, however, imagine that he is suffering a real injury, for to develop that habit is a vice." To this second-century Roman, grief is an indulgence and a waste of energy.

In the final paragraphs of his *Meditations*, the stoic philosopher recalls the regret we all feel as our life comes to a close. As actors in a cosmic drama, we rebel against an early curtain: "But I have not played the five acts, but only three." Then nature answers us: "You have played well, but in your life at any rate the three acts are the whole play." If we would accept our fate, we would find no reason to grieve and no cause for anger. For Marcus Aurelius, the negative emotions are interior, fruitless disturbances. We do well to banish these passions that distract us from a calm and serene life.

Marcus Aurelius died in the year 180, just as a young Christian by the name of Clement arrived in the North African metropolis of Alexandria. As head of a Christian study center, Clement developed a spirituality combining religious and civic virtues. Stoicism provided Clement with the vocabulary for this task.

In his guide for Christian living, Clement's instructions ranged from table manners (one should exhibit "no indecorum in the act of swallowing") to public bathing (permitted for purposes of hygiene, but not pleasure). Clement's ideal of quelling disruptive emotions was expressed in the stoic term *Apatheia*. For Clement *apatheia* did not mean a lethargic "apathy," but a blissful deliverance from the interior whirlwinds of rage, panic, and grief.

Peter Brown, in his magisterial work *Body and Society*, reminds us of the special meaning of "passions" for Clement. These were distorted emotions that "colored perceptions of the outside world with nonexistent sources of fear, anxiety or hope; or else they bathed it in a false glow of pleasure and potential satisfaction." Emotions like sadness or sexual desire easily shroud us in toxic vapors. "If undispersed by vigilant reflection, such vapors could mist over the entire inner climate of the mind, wrapping it in a thick fog of 'passions.'"

For Marcus Aurelius and Clement, passions were bodily impulses at constant cross purposes with our spiritual aspirations. Emotion and reason jousted for control of the person; the soul pined for a haven removed from the disruptions of anger, grief, and sexual passion. Clement, like other stoic writers, appealed to Plato's image of the charioteer and his horses: human reason must rein in and master the untamed passions. This dualism of emotion and reason, of flesh and spirit, still haunts Christian efforts to forge a robust spirituality of the emotional life.

The negative emotions continue to scandalize Christians. Many of us still harbor the ideal that maturity means serenity and that holiness requires the mastery of emotions. The Christian community is challenged today to forge a spirituality in which our emotions are recognized as more than private passions to be silenced by private remedies. Instead, we need to reimagine our passions as social instincts that link us with one another and alert us to our cherished values. We must decipher the mysterious chemistry through which bodily impulses ignite spiritual insight and the alchemy by which reason and emotion embrace.

A Knife over the Heart

A spirituality of the negative emotions will be anchored in the difficult virtue of patience. As painful feelings of anger or fear or loneliness threaten our calm and control, we are tempted to flee the emotion. The Chinese character for patience urges us to endure the threat until we learn its mission. The character represents a knife poised over a heart. Is this an assassin's sword or a surgeon's healing blade? "Should I flee to avoid this sinister attack? Or stay, opening myself to a painful purification that may save my life?" Patience is the ability to hold still under threat, until we can discern what is at stake.

Patience demands neither passivity nor docility, but a fierce attentiveness to what is really happening. The medieval philosopher Thomas Aquinas observed that patience girds us "to endure immediate injuries in such a way as not to be unduly dejected by them." Unlike the stoics, Aquinas believed that sadness (*tristitia*) is an ordinary and honorable part of life. But sadness quickly spirals into melancholy and depression. Patience equips us to hold our hurt in a way that blocks this destructive escalation. For Aquinas, patience is one of the faces of fortitude: courage to live life to the fullest requires our willingness to face the sorrows and losses that accumulate along the way. Aquinas judges: "through patience a person possesses her soul."

But something in the American character does not like patience. A culture of ambition makes it difficult for us to hold still. Patience seems to put a damper on the spontaneity and freedom that we so cherish. Too much introspection unsettles our national soul. Faced with problems and scandals, our leaders encourage us—impatiently—"to put it behind us" and move on. A consumer society's dependence on impulse buying and the media's accommodation to short attention spans do not foster the development of patience. Advertising campaigns in which sports celebrities urge us "Just do it!" celebrate athletes' spontaneous grace while ignoring the disciplined patience that perfected these skills.

Befriending the negative emotions demands patience. Patience prepares us to live our life wide awake; to taste our negative emotions, rather than swallowing our pain. In the chapters ahead we will explore the disciplines of patience that transform our negative emotions into positive passions for life.

Reflective Exercise

Select one negative emotion that is important for you now and recall a recent experience of this emotion's arousal.

- What was the situation that evoked this emotion for you?
- How did your body respond?
- What other feelings accompanied this emotion here?

Now consider the different *cultures* that have helped shape your experience of this emotion.

A. How was this emotion handled in your *family* as you were growing up? Give an example, to help make your reflection more concrete. Is there a word, phrase, or image that best captures the way that your family dealt with this emotion?

B. How has your *church and religious tradition* influenced you? Can you recall a person, story, or teaching in the church that has helped you with this emotion? Can you recall a way in which your religious tradition has hindered or frustrated you in regard to this emotion?

C. How has your national *culture* (U.S., Canadian, Australian, Asian, etc.) influenced your judgments about this emotion? For example, in the society you know best, how is a "good woman" (or a "good man") supposed to deal with this emotion? What other influences on your emotional life have you felt from your culture?

Additional Resources

Amy Clampitt's poem "The Field Pansy" appears in her recent collection *Westward*. Clifford Geertz discusses the perilous flexibility of the human species in *The Interpretation of Cultures*; we quote from p. 99. Joseph Pieper explores Thomas Aquinas's understanding of patience in *The Four Cardinal Virtues*.

For an introduction to current psychological research on cultural influences and cultural differences in emotional life, see *Emotions and Culture*, edited by Shinobu Kitayama and Hazel Markus. Carol Zisowitz Stearns and Peter N. Stearns document "the overwhelming power that society has over individuals in giving them the very language by which they appraise situations and judge their responses" (p. 218) in *Anger: The Struggle for Emotional Control in American History*. Arlie Russell Hochschild analyzes the ways contemporary U.S. culture continues to shape emotion in *The Managed Heart: Commercialization of Human Feeling*. F.G. Bailey discusses the political uses of emotion, especially anger, in *The Tactical Uses of Passion*.

In his book *Vanquished Nation, Broken Spirit: The Virtues of the Heart in Formative Judaism*, Jacob Neusner acknowledges the influence of philosopher Robert Solomon. Neusner stresses the social constructionist view of feelings, insisting that emotions are "an aspect of culture, something learned, handed down, and therefore constructed, not private, not personal, not individual. Emotions are traditions" (p. 10). Earl Shorris explores the feeling range of *aguantar* in his *Latinos: A Biography of the People*; see pp. 92, 105, 311, 377, and 433.

Roberto Unger discusses boredom in *Passion: An Essay on Personality*; we quote from pp. 112–113. For a wider ranging exploration of the epidemic of boredom in American life, see Sam Keen's *Inward Bound*. We are indebted to philosopher Paul Ricoeur's rich study of the imagery of failure and guilt in *The Symbolism of Evil*.

In *Body and Society: Men, Women, and Sexual Renunciation in Early Christianity*, Peter Brown traces the intriguing link between turning from sexuality and turning from society, in monasticism and other forms of Christian asceticism; see pp. 129 and 130 for his comments on the meaning of "passions." The Greek text of Marcus Aurelius's *The Meditations* is available in the Loeb Classical Library Edition; we quote here from G.N.A. Grube's translation, pp. 66, 79, and 129.

Clement of Alexandria wrote two main collections of works. For selections from the *Stromata* on marriage, see vol. II of *Alexandrian Christianity*, edited by Henry Chadwick. His pedagogical primer is only available in *Clément d'Alexandrie: Le Pédagogue*, vol. 158 in the *Sources Chrétiennes* series, edited by M. Harl; for Clement's discussion of food, see chapter 1; for laughter, chapter 5; for bathing, chapter 9. See also Salvatore Lilla's *Clement of Alexandria*, p. 95 for observations on Clement's dualism; on p. 96 Lilla recalls Clement's judgment that the passions "are the worst disease of the soul."

Part Two

ANGER—
THE EMERGENCY
EMOTION

The Chinese character ch'i
signifies vital human energy
and this energy expressed as anger

4

Tracking the Tigers of Wrath

It is dawn in China. In public parks and rural fields
throughout this vast country, people young and old gather to
pace themselves through the rhythmic movements of an ancient discipline, *t'ai ch'i*. The simple choreography of this
classic exercise regime—part martial art, part oriental
ballet—brings body and mind to alertness. The mysterious
and healing energy of *ch'i* begins to flow.

In the elusive language of China, *ch'i* stands for spirit, energy, and
arousal. The core figure in the written Chinese character is "rice
coming to boil in a pot." This suggestive image—the water's agitation
as the temperature rises, the necessary risk of boiling over in order to
transform the dry seed into nourishing food, the abundant increase of
the rice as it cooks—resists easy translation. Chinese scholar Lee Yearley identifies *ch'i* as the physiological and spiritual energy that stimulates us toward vital self-expression. *Ch'i* is evident in our "animated"
conversation, in our "spirited" pursuit of an ideal or goal. *Ch'i* also
rises when our anger (*sheng ch'i*) is aroused.

The Chinese language designates in this single word both the fundamental energy of our humanity and the volatile emotion of our wrath.
The arousal that sometimes boils over in rage also fuels our determination. If we could surgically remove *ch'i* we might never get angry, but
we would lack the critical energy on which courageous action depends.

Anger is the most frequent of the negative emotions. This familiar
companion shows itself as a flash of irritation, a peevish complaint, a
simmering sense of indignation. Unattended, anger's everyday arousal
may sink into a harbored resentment or sour into a longing for retaliation and revenge.

Among North Americans, these angry feelings are almost always seen as negative. Culturally we're instructed that being angry isn't cool—"Don't get mad; get even." Morally we've been cautioned that anger is one of the seven deadly sins. We've learned, too, that being angry isn't good for our health; anger raises blood pressure, interferes with digestion, strains the immune system. We fear its social consequences even more. Anger sets us at odds with those we love. When angry behavior turns brutal, people are hurt and relationships destroyed. Rage stokes America's epidemic of incivility and violence. So we conclude: Anger feels bad and has bad effects.

But that's not the whole story. Consider another experience that gives us pause: the common inability to become angry. Many Americans have great difficulty with conflict. Eager to please, we flash uncertain smiles in the face of disagreement. Our hunger to belong works against any willingness to confront controversy. Summoning the energy to defend our values or to address an affront seems out-of-bounds. For many of us caught in this cultural mood, the memory of Jesus angrily driving the money changers from the holy place of prayer comes as a challenge to our own cowardice. This biblical image reminds us there are values worth fighting for and threats to which we must respond.

Three centuries before Jesus, Aristotle described anger as the energy that enables us to face difficulty. The "good tempered" person is able to draw on this energy—to become angry when injustices arise. If too much anger threatens to erupt in destructive violence, too little puts us at risk as well. Deprived of this volatile energy we are unable to stand up to provocation; instead, in Aristotle's words, we "put up with an insult to oneself or suffer one's friend to be insulted." Such a lack of spirit undermines our engagement in life.

Thomas Aquinas, the medieval philosopher who brought Aristotle's thought into the mainstream of Christian culture, expanded this optimistic vision of anger. For Aquinas, feeling angry is normal: "It is natural . . . to be aroused against what is hostile and threatening." Anger's irritation serves us well since it stirs us to "repulse an injury and seek vindication." In the end, anger's arousal may provoke courage, for anger is "a disturbance of the heart to remove a threat to what one loves."

Anger, then, is a signal serving our survival. Its arousal urges us to defend ourselves, our interests, our values. In psychiatrist Willard Gaylin's words, anger "arms and alarms," alerting us to threat and energizing us to act. And beyond self-defense, anger serves social transformation. Theologian Beverly Wildung Harrison reminds us, "We must never lose touch with the fact that all serious moral activity, especially action for social change, takes its bearings from the rising power of human anger."

Anger's Arousal

The body serves notice when we get mad. But, intriguingly, we don't all feel the same. Most people become tense but others report numbness. People may break out in a sweat or develop chills along with goose bumps. Changes in skin temperature make some faces flush while others grow pale.

Across these different experiences, the underlying physiological process is the same. Our bodies are being readied for "fight or flight." Adrenal hormones course through the body, arousing us to alert. Heartbeat and breathing rates accelerate, blood pressure increases, skeletal muscles tense. The mind, too, is affected. Moderate hormonal increases sharpen our attention, but high adrenal levels sustained over a long time lead to confusion and exhaustion.

Physically, anger readies us to confront a crisis at hand. Digestion slows as blood supply is diverted from the digestive organs, to bring additional oxygen and other nutrients to the muscles and the brain. These changes maximize strength, increase stamina, and heighten concentration—preparing us for urgent response.

But the *feeling* of anger involves more than this set of physical reactions; being angry includes judgments about what these reactions *mean*. The hormones that put the body on alert can be stimulated by a range of factors: physical exercise or injury; drugs like caffeine and nicotine; an environment that is stressful or unfamiliar; a family quarrel or a traffic jam. And researchers report that similar states of physiological arousal occur in several emotions. So distinguishing fear from anger, or anxiety from eager anticipation, is not easy if we follow only biological cues.

Being angry involves a state of physiological arousal *and* an interpretation of what this arousal means. As an emotion, then, anger *is* this complex experience of arousal-and-interpretation. An example may help.

I am waiting in line in a crowded supermarket. Balancing my several purchases in my arms (I was in too big a hurry to get a cart), I wait for those in front of me to move through the checkout line. As I wait, the person behind me jostles me. Edging forward, I bump the person in front, who responds with a cold look. I am becoming aroused and the name I give to this feeling is anger. Blaming the checkout person, the rabble around me, and myself (for coming at such a busy time), I identify my escalating distress as anger.

Later that day, having survived the trip to the supermarket, I head out for the football game at a nearby university. As I approach the stadium I fall in with the throng hurrying to their seats. At the stadium itself I find myself jostled and moved along by the large crowd. There are smiles all around, along with chatter about the weather and comments about our team's chances for victory. I am aroused and I like it. Here the jostling and the crush of people, similar to but even worse than at the market, stimulates me. This arousal, interpreted differently, becomes not anger but a delightful anticipation.

A state of arousal accompanies most emotions—not just anger. And whether this aroused state is named anger or something else depends not only on what is happening in the body but what is going on in the mind—on the judgments we make about our experience. Before exploring the judgments that are part of our experience of anger, we must recall its favorite sites.

The Arenas of Anger

"Anger is a highly interpersonal emotion," psychologist James Averill insists, "emerg[ing] at the interface of self and society. It cannot be fully understood apart from the social contexts in which it occurs." Three social contexts account for our most frequent experiences of anger—close relationships, public exchange, and settings where justice is at stake.

Intimate Anger

> Anger is not the opposite of love. . . . Anger is a mode of connectedness and it is always a vivid form of caring.
>
> *Beverly Wildung Harrison*

Our close relationships teach us that anger and affection are no strangers. In fact, the people we love are most able to drive us crazy!

Anger toward intimates is most frequent because we spend so much time together. Where lives intersect and activities overlap, we are likely to get in each other's way. Intimate anger is most significant because these relationships matter most: With spouse and family members, among friends or work colleagues, angry behavior has far-reaching consequences. Expressing anger to someone close can make things better between us—or much worse. And intimate anger is most threatening because we know one another's vulnerabilities. Up close, we so easily bruise the sore spots—the sensitive issues that wound one another, the hot topics that provoke our rage.

Maturity brings us to recognize anger as inevitably intimacy's companion—and even part of its strength. "Anger is aroused when a significant relationship is threatened," Dana Crowley Jack notes, "and its goal is to promote, not disrupt the relationship." Psychologist Rochelle Albin goes further; "Anger," she says, "can be a constructive emotion that helps resolve hurts and differences between people, improves their understanding of one another, and gives their relationship a firmer base." But to reap these benefits, we must learn to handle anger well.

In close relationships, resolving anger often requires a direct approach—acknowledging our mutual distress, confronting together the issues that rankle, working out solutions we can live with, learning to forgive. But many of us are reluctant to deal directly with intimate anger. Afraid of driving away those we depend on, we hesitate to admit anger toward people close to us. Yet experience shows that to talk it out and work it through often leads to deeper understanding and greater commitment in a relationship. Resolving intimate anger usually demands that we first acknowledge to ourselves that we are angry. Then we need to approach the other person involved, so that we can confront the concern together and work toward some practical solution.

Public Anger

> Fear and anger were designed to serve as responses to threats to our survival. To our *survival*—not to our pride, status, position, manhood or dignity.
>
> *Willard Gaylin*

Anger surges in impersonal settings as well. Sometimes getting through the day is downright difficult: a car pulls ahead of us in heavy traffic; a computer error on our bank statement resists correction; a loud party runs late in the neighborhood. Inconveniences like these multiply in a complex, fast-paced society. If we interpret these inevitable slights as intentional provocations—"they're out to get me"—anger erupts.

Taking action can reduce the arousal we feel in response to the assaults and strains of modern life. A commitment to reducing stress in our own lives helps: simplifying our daily schedule, learning to say "no," enlarging our vision so that we see fewer people as enemies. Often practical assertion is required—returning defective merchandise, calling the contractor to insure that a scheduled repair project is completed on time, negotiating with an adjoining property-owner to settle a problem between us. Our intent in these transactions is not to deepen a friendship or to preserve a close working relationship. The more modest goal is a return to public civility.

Public anger is often a barometer of the other tensions in our lives. Recall how irritable we are on days when busy schedules leave us physically taxed and emotionally drained. The agitation that comes with continuing stress primes us for anger. Living through a bitter divorce or confronted with a threatened job loss, people find themselves responding with hostility in circumstances that otherwise they could cope with calmly. And current studies into the roots of urban violence point to more than the increasing availability of deadly weapons. Jeffrey Fagan of the School of Criminal Justice at Rutgers University underscores the links between violent young people and the staggering harshness of their daily experience. The cumulative stress from day-to-day interactions that regularly evoke fear and contempt results—for many inner-city children—in a state of heightened physiological arousal. Even small provocations can turn this arousal into violent response.

Dealing with public anger means finding ways to manage the inevitable friction of social interaction—strategies that help us develop tolerance toward one another and learn to mediate our disputes. Paradoxically, resolving this public distress frequently requires a focus on ourselves—the disciplines of overcoming our impatience, turning away from provocation, and getting on with our lives.

Justice Anger

Anger is the necessary handmaiden of sympathy and fairness.
James Q. Wilson

Anger also flares in the face of injustice—unfair treatment of us or "our kind," actions that attack our sense of decency or fair play, situations that show contempt for values at the core of our own world-view. When we are confronted by injustice, anger fuels our commitment to right the wrong. But anger at injustice can misfire, provoking behaviors that are self-destructive or target the wrong enemy. A telling example: The Los Angeles fires and looting that followed the verdict in the first trial of police accused in the Rodney King beating devastated the neighborhood in which the rioters themselves lived, taking the biggest toll on the local businesses that provided basic services and jobs in the community.

African American theologian Cornel West probes deeply for the roots of this kind of violence, finding them in the unremitting assaults that racism mounts on black consciousness. "The accumulated effect of these wounds and scars produces a deep-seated anger, a boiling sense of rage, and a passionate pessimism regarding America's will to justice." While pundits and politicians cite unbridled anger as the cause of such urban violence, a growing number of thoughtful analysts concur with West's judgment that the more dangerous dynamic is nihilism: "the monumental eclipse of hope, the unprecedented collapse of meaning, the incredible disregard of human (especially black) life." West calls for a *politics of conversion* to arouse disheartened communities from their collective depression and engage them once again in the struggle for social equality. In pursuit of this national conversion, justice anger helps keep hope alive.

Systemic injustice seldom yields to short-term solutions. In these intractable settings, anger needs to be both nurtured and tempered. Here group support is critical. Riot response committees formed in the local churches of South-Central Los Angeles, nationwide chapters of Mothers Against Drunk Driving, women's political action groups that emerged after the 1992 Anita Hill/Clarence Thomas hearings, the movement of basic Christian communities in Latin America and the Philippines—these are places where the resilient anger of justice is forged. Supportive gatherings like this protect people from simply being overwhelmed by their feelings of frustration and rage. But the group's goal is not getting rid of anger but keeping its energy alive. Coming together renews conviction in the justice of our cause. In the safety of this setting, volatile emotions can be expressed, confirmed, and focused into effective action. Justice anger, carefully cultivated, sustains us through the lengthy processes of clarifying common goals, developing a plan of action, overcoming setbacks, and celebrating even modest gains.

Identifying Chronic Anger

Bitterness is like cancer. It eats upon the host. But anger is like fire. It burns it all clear.

Maya Angelou

In each of these social settings, anger is an emergency emotion—provoked by sudden threat, resolved by swift response. Anger's painful urgency compels us to act quickly in self-defense. After we respond to the danger, our body calms and the sense of urgency subsides. With the emergency met, we are released from anger's hold. We feel relieved, sometimes even renewed.

But things don't always work out this way. Our angry feelings sometimes resolve quickly, but often they continue to smolder. The emergency emotion deteriorates into a chronic mood; we experience ourselves as angry all the time.

In his discussion of anger, Aristotle observes that "the bitter tempered . . . remain angry for a long *time* [*chronos*; chronic] because they keep their wrath inside." Rather than seizing the opportunity to either act on this emotion or actively turn away from its demands, these persons indulge themselves in anger. Feeling hurt or offended, they nurse their feelings in private. As Aristotle observes, "Because their anger is concealed, no one else tries to placate them." Since people who hide their anger often seem calm and in control, other people do not sense their wrath—at least not at first. But soon this privatized distress starts to corrode their public calm and their anger leaks out as sarcasm or contempt. Since the bitterness of chronically angry people seems so disconnected from any obvious offense, bystanders can't understand their anger. Often the angry persons themselves aren't sure of the cause.

Chronic anger sometimes dresses up as resentment. Feeling resentful, we privately rehearse our grievances: we picture ourselves insulting those who have offended us, stopping them in their tracks with a cutting remark. We indulge ourselves in blaming others, but all the action takes place in the private theater of our heart. Robert Solomon suggests that resentment is anger defeated by authority. Resentful of powerful figures in our life, we feel too inferior to confront them directly. Resentment is anger ashamed to show its face. But this feeling does show its face—in the corrosive guise of sarcasm and bitter re-marks. These actions release some of the pent up energy of our internal rage but never relieve the hurt. Compelled to repeat our hostile or snide observations, we gradually pollute our own environment. Chronic anger slowly consumes us and drives our companions away.

Chronic anger assumes other disguises, as well. Passive aggression, in which we both comply and show our frustrated resistance, reveals an unhealthy face of anger. The habitual use of irony may be the educated person's expression of chronic anger. The central figure in Wallace Stegner's novel *All the Little Live Things* uncovers his own mask of irony:

> Sympathy I have failed in, stoicism I have barely passed. But I have made straight A in irony—that curse, that evasion, that armor, that way of staying safe while seeming wise.

Resentment and sarcasm often result from our judgment that expressing anger directly is too dangerous. This leads us to examine how we appraise our anger.

Anger's Appraisal

Anger carries a moral claim: A wrong has been done that should be set right. This claim is not always accurate. Often enough following our immediate feelings misleads us; conclusions we rush to in anger must be revised later, when a calmer mood prevails. Since anger's appraisals are judgment calls, its judgments need to be tested. But testing our anger does not demand dismissing its claims out of hand. Rather we must learn to read, to review, to reevaluate the judgments our anger makes.

Injury Received

Anger's first judgment is of injury received. Physical injury makes us mad: a car door slams on my hand, a neighborhood bully threatens bodily harm. More often the injury is to our self-esteem. Norman Rohrer and Philip Sutherland speak of anger as a hedge against humili-ation. Insults and ridicule come as personal attacks, damaging our self-respect. Being belittled threatens to diminish us in our own eyes. But as self-esteem starts to slip away, another emotion often intervenes. Offended, we get angry. And our anger interrupts the downward spiral of self-doubt. Other interpretations arise: "I don't deserve this abuse. You can't treat me this way!" Those who work with battered women, for example, report that this angry affirmation marks a turning point in a woman's recovery from the cycle of abuse.

Sometimes the injury is to our worldview, our confident sense of how reality works. When people challenge our values, when events call into question our basic assumptions, when others flaunt the rules we honor, anger flares. The risk here goes deeper than "I may be wrong." These affronts threaten our meaning-world, the certainties that help us make sense of life. What triggers the anger may be significant: recall the anger throughout this country in the early 1970s over the stalemate in Vietnam, threatening as it did the loss of America's privileged position in the world. Or seemingly small: remember the anger generated in the 1960s over transgressions of dress code that seem almost trivial today—women wearing pant suits to the office or men letting their hair grow long. Whatever the trigger, anger is provoked when the established order and our own secure place in it are at risk.

Accusation of Blame

A second appraisal—anger accuses. Assigning responsibility is at the heart of anger. "More than anything else," James Averill remarks, "anger is an attribution of blame." Harm has been done and someone must be held accountable. We may fault ourselves (anger at self is a big part of feeling guilty) or someone else. Often enough we assign blame inaccurately: innocent bystanders—even inanimate objects—stand mistakenly accused. But finding a culprit is part of what it means to be angry.

Anger flares when we are frustrated—denied something we need; blocked from something we want; prevented from reaching our goal. Under stress we personalize the frustration, interpreting interference as a direct assault. "The careless bus driver is out to get me." "The evil genius who lives inside my computer has selected me for special suffering."

Harboring anger is hard without someone to blame. When we recognize no one is really at fault, anger dissipates. We may still feel annoyed at the situation. We may still be inconvenienced by what has happened or irritated by what was done, but we are unlikely to remain angry. Consider a couple of examples.

In the shopping mall someone bumps us from behind, dislodging our packages and scattering their contents. We turn with an angry rebuke, to find that the person behind us has tripped and fallen. Our anger turns to concern. "Are you all right?" we ask as we rush to offer our assistance.

In this situation we have been genuinely inconvenienced: we've been knocked about, our packages are on the floor in disarray, our plans have been interrupted. We probably feel annoyed: all these people crowding around are just adding to the confusion! And we quickly become impatient: why haven't the mall security people arrived to offer assistance? We may even be looking for someone to blame: why don't they pay more attention to the floors on the wet days? But, judging that she is not really responsible, we're not likely to remain angry at the person who actually fell on us.

Anger also loses its hold when we learn that the person we blame is not really the culprit.

> My neighbor is late returning a borrowed chainsaw. When I spoke to him yesterday, mentioning my plan to spend this afternoon clearing the yard of storm debris, he agreed to return it by noon today. Turning to the task this afternoon, I check the garage. The chainsaw is nowhere to be found. My anger mounts. I fume, accusing the neighbor of being inconsiderate (and worse), and stomp into the house to give him a call. Just then my son Greg rushes from his room, the saw in his hand. My neighbor, true to his word, had stopped by earlier. Finding the garage door locked (I had assured him it would be open!) he stopped at the front door and left the saw with my son. Greg, busy with his own schedule, brought it to his room, forgetting it was there until he heard my rantings in the yard. When I learn these details, my anger toward my neighbor disappears. I'm tempted to shout at Greg for not getting the saw to me sooner. Happily, I catch myself in time. Responsibility for this mix-up is mainly mine; I'm the one who forgot to leave the garage open. I'm embarrassed by the slipup, and a bit angry at myself for all the fuss.

Assertive Response

A third appraisal: Anger urges us to act. Being angry brings a realization that we can, we should, we must respond now. In some situations, this urgency serves us poorly. We act before we have considered the consequences—striking out in violence or taking foolish risks. But anger's insistence also fortifies us for a more effective response.

Anger commits us to action. The links between anger and action are sufficiently strong so that if someone says "this makes me angry" but makes no attempt to change the offending situation, we doubt they are really angry.

Being angry empowers us—body and mind. A friend of ours captures the experience well: "When I am angry I feel strong!" Physically, anger generates energy. Being angry mobilizes our body for vigorous action, so we actually feel tougher. Psychologically, anger builds confidence. Being angry bolsters the sense that *we are right*. Doubts fall away in face of the conviction our complaints are valid and our actions justified. The awareness that "I must do something" grows. Sometimes "doing something" goes only as far as letting off steam: we curse our lot or shout out accusations or stalk away, slamming the door as we leave. But "doing something" becomes more constructive when we move to remedy the harmful situation.

Anger provokes a passionate response: we act on our convictions, press for justice, try to instigate change. Such assertive actions make claims, inserting us into the thick of things. But anger's assertion does not necessarily lead to aggressive behavior. In fact, by drawing attention to the problem early and giving us time to work out a suitable solution before things get too bad, assertion usually works to prevent aggressive attack.

Aggression involves direct attack intended to bring harm. In his research into the everyday experience of anger, psychologist James Averill discovered that the links between anger and aggressive behavior are not strong. Even when they are angry, most people consider a direct attack on the blameworthy culprit to be a tactic of last resort. More typically, angry people try to communicate convictions (*This is important!*), to defend rights (*I deserve better!*), to indict misdeeds (*What is happening here is wrong!*). Their anger prompts vigorous action to correct a bad situation. This kind of assertion brings feelings of personal empowerment. Violence is more likely to result in settings where people felt impotent, without effective ways to express their anger or to use its energy to make things better.

A Sense of Hope

Finally, being angry carries the conviction that something *can* be done. This hope makes anger a friend of transformation, an honorable dynamic in change and growth. Most therapists know anger is an ally; its energy fuels the hard work of personal change. Harriet Goldhur Lerner of the Menninger Clinic, whose influential work has redefined the experience of anger for women, notes that "anger should be used to define a new position in a relationship pattern, a position that does not mean self-betrayal." Many marriage counselors, in fact, prefer working with couples who are angry. People who are angry with one another are still significant in each other's lives. Indifference is a greater enemy of reconciliation than is anger, because angry people are still linked.

Anger signals social transformation as well. Angry people want things to be different; their anger says NO to the status quo. Angry demands arise from the hope that change is possible. When people lose this hope, anger dies. This connection makes anger crucial in social change. People long oppressed become resigned to their fate. Passive in the face of their plight, they are reluctant to work for change. "What's the use; nothing can be done; this is just the way things are." But anger brings a sense of entitlement—"We deserve better!" Feeling entitled, people rally to action—standing up to challenges, pressing for change, promoting reform. So community organizers and other advocates of change do not shy away from the distress of anger. "We're trying to give people back their anger, because anger will give them back their hope."

Anger remains an unpleasant and unsettling emotion. It threatens our self-control and overturns our serenity. Most of us would much prefer to live without it. But anger is a necessary disturbance. When we are belittled, when our values are threatened, when injustice imperils our shared life, we must be able to be aroused against these offenses. Befriended and tamed, anger becomes the powerful ally of our responsible life in the world.

Reflective Exercise

Recall a recent time when you were angry with someone else. Spend a few moments bringing the incident to mind: what triggered your anger toward this person? Did you express your anger? If so, how? If not, why? What happened as a result?

Now consider this incident in terms of gains and losses. Were there any *gains* resulting from this experience—positive results, benefits received, good effects? List whatever comes to mind. Were there any *losses* experienced here—negative results, harm inflicted, bad effects? Again, let your response range widely.

Next, recall a time when you were the target of someone else's anger. Let yourself be present to the experience again: as you see it, what triggered the anger toward you? How was it expressed? How did you feel? What happened as a result of this angry exchange? Then consider this incident in terms of *gains* and *losses*, using the questions in the paragraph above as a guide.

Finally, spend a few moments comparing your assessment of these two examples of anger. What learnings do you take away from this reflection, to influence your experience of anger in the future?

Additional Resources

Psychologist James R. Averill has made significant contributions to the understanding of everyday anger; see his book *Anger and Aggression* and the later article "Studies on Anger and Aggression: Implications for Theories of Emotion"; in this chapter we quote from pp. 1149 and 1150 in the article. Theologian Beverly Wildung Harrison discusses the positive potential of anger in "The Place of Anger in the Works of Love" in *Making the Connections: Essays in Feminist Social Ethics*, edited by Carol S. Robb; we quote twice from p. 14. In *Good Anger*, philosopher Giles Milhaven argues for a reexamination of the positive role of "vindictive" anger.

In *The Dance of Anger*, Harriet Goldhur Lerner writes perceptively about the benefits and abuses of intimate anger. Looking especially at women's experience, she suggests practical ways to break unhealthy patterns of angry response. Thomas Tyrrell demonstrates anger's importance in maturing relationships in *The Adventure of Intimacy: A Journey through Broken Circles*. In her larger analysis of depression, *Silencing the Self*, Dana Crowley Jack examines the valuable contribution anger makes to the effort of personal and social change; we quote from p. 41.

Willard Gaylin offers a comprehensive look at anger as an emergency emotion often at odds with the complex demands of contemporary life in *The Rage Within: Anger in Modern Life*. James Q. Wilson urges recognition of the moral sensitivities needed to moderate current society's rampant hostility in *The Moral Sense*; Richard Mouw, in *Uncommon Decency: Christian Civility in an Uncivil World*, challenges the religious community to assume leadership in returning tolerance and respect to the discourse of public debate. In *Words Made Flesh: Scripture, Psychology and Human Communication*, Fran Ferder makes practical recommendations for communicating well in contexts of anger and conflict.

Cornel West examines "Nihilism in Black America" in his *Race Matters*: we quote from p. 224; see also his *Keeping Faith: Philosophy and Race in America*. For details of Jeffrey Fagan's research on urban violence, see Michel Marriott's article "On Meaner Streets, the Violent Are More So," *New York Times* (September 13, 1992). Maya Angelou's distinction between anger and bitterness is part of her interview in *Writing Lives: Conversations between Women Writers*. Wallace Stegner's comment on irony is found in *All the Little Live Things*, p. 12.

For discussion of the debilitating effects of chronic anger and practical strategies for overcoming them see: *Anger Kills* by Virginia and Redford Williams; *When Anger Hurts: Quieting the Storm Within* by Matthew McKay, Peter Rogers and Judith McKay; *Facing Anger* by Norman Rohrer and Philip Sutherland; and *Our Inner World of Rage* by Lucy Freeman.

Lee Yearley examines *ch'i* as a "psychophysical energy" with "numinous qualities" that, in Mencius, is intimately related to righteousness and courage; see his *Mencius and Aquinas: Theories of Virtue and Conceptions of Courage*, especially pp. 152–54. For Aristotle's discussion of anger, see *Nicomachean Ethics* 1125B–1126B. Thomas Aquinas's observations on anger are found in Questions 46–48 of Ia–IIae of his *Summa Theologiae*.

5

Women and Men: Learning Anger's Rules

People everywhere get angry, but they get angry in the service of their culture's rules. Sometimes those rules are explicit
. . . ; more often they are implicit, disguised in the countless
daily actions performed because "That's the way we do things
around here."

Carol Tavris

Do women and men follow different rules for anger? The question
of gender differences arises early in most discussions of anger.
Do men and women stand apart in the ways they experience or express
this basic emotion? Or does a common humanity unite us here? Answers these days come from several quarters.

Sociobiologists argue that evolution equips men for attack, making
anger more appropriate for the male of the species. Scientists studying
animals cannot ask their subjects about their inner experience of feeling
angry, so these researchers focus instead on aggressive behavior. Their
argument goes this way: Among primates, males are larger, stronger
and more aggressive than females. Among humans, too, males tend
to be larger and stronger. Therefore, men are inherently inclined to
aggressive behavior and, by inference, more prone to anger.

Psychologists studying anger directly, however, report few consistent
differences between women and men. Looking at how people respond
to real-life situations, for example, James Averill and William Frost
conclude that "empirical research lends little support to the notion
that women are less prone to anger than men are or that women are
more inhibited in their expression of anger." Subsequent research has

confirmed these results. From individual to individual, of course, people differ in how they deal with anger. But these differences don't fall along gender lines. As a group, women tend to get angry for the same reasons as men do and they show their anger in roughly the same ways. For example: Men and women alike get angry most frequently with people closest to them. Unfair treatment and lack of consideration are the main triggers of anger for both women and men. And men and women agree that anger can have positive results (improving a bad situation, strengthening a relationship) as well as negative consequences (hurting oneself or others, making matters worse).

In these North American studies, only two gender differences showed up regularly: as a group, men are more likely to express anger in public. And many women, but few men, report being moved to tears by their anger. How to explain these differences? It's more likely, say the researchers, that these contrasts result from social prohibitions (women are expected not to be assertive in public; men are not supposed to cry) than from any "natural" difference between the sexes. Carol Tavris summarizes these research findings: "Neither sex has a special difficulty in expressing anger. But both sexes have trouble with anger."

While these empirical studies seem to downplay differences between women and men in anger, a significant number of social scientists and feminist thinkers—both women and men—continue to explore the impact of gender. These analysts share the conviction that gender differences are rooted in power differences. In most social settings in our society—family life, education, employment, religion, the political arena—men and women occupy different levels of power. These power discrepancies make a difference in how women and men deal with anger.

This difference appears starkly in how society evaluates angry men and angry women. A man who speaks in anger is often seen as passionately committed to his cause, as authentically expressing his deepest conviction. So anger enhances his credibility. But an angry woman, Harriet Lerner reminds us, remains generally unacceptable to American society. Even in this era of women's acknowledged public achievement, being angry tends to invalidate what a woman says. She is seen as too emotional or too strident, as irrational or over-involved. By showing anger a woman undermines her credibility—and makes people mad.

Jean Baker Miller and her colleagues at the Stone Center of Wellesley College provide a compelling analysis of the social influences that define anger for women and men. Anger is an essential human response, signaling something is wrong and motivating us to remedy the situation. Many forces in U.S. society constantly provoke angry *feelings*—our competitiveness, our consumerism, a commitment to individualism that tempts us to view other people as adversaries. At the same time, our culture works hard to curb any *expression* of this anger. Both men and women feel pressured by these cultural proscriptions. But, as Miller demonstrates, the "constraints for women are different, and more restrictive than those for men." These contrasting rules about anger, drawn along gender lines, shape different emotional experiences.

Women's World of Anger

In our society—in most societies—women live with secondary status. The roles and responsibilities open to them tend to be seen as essential but subordinate. Growing up, girls gradually become aware of these limits of being female. Simply because they are women, many benefits widely prized in their society—leadership, influence, independence, power, prestige, wealth—are less available to them.

Since anger is a normal response to perceived injustice, one might expect that a group continually deprived like this would have good reason to be angry. But people who benefit from the unequal power arrangement are loath for such anger to develop. Recognizing that widespread discontent might threaten the status quo, they takes steps to outlaw anger ahead of time. Physical force can be used to stifle disruption, but more effective is to have subordinates stifle themselves. So most cultures, serving the interests of the dominant group, instruct members of subordinate groups to interpret their anger not as a legitimate response to injustice but as "my problem." As a personal problem, anger should be kept out of sight. Better, it should be overcome.

This social pressure to inhibit anger touches members of many marginal groups—poor people, members of ethnic minorities, those who are sexually marginalized—as well as women. But cultural definitions of femininity *reinforce* the sense that anger is illegitimate for women. The "ideal" woman's energy is directed beyond herself. She is giver of new life, nurturer of the sick, educator of the young, supporter of worthy causes. Her rightful place is at the heart of the family network where, as dutiful daughter, faithful wife, self-effacing mother, she stands on call to other people's needs. In the public world, she takes these feminine graces with her: supporting her boss, championing his career, doing the gritty work of a thousand thankless tasks, and accepting lower pay for the privilege. This image of femininity leaves little room for anger's assertive demands. The "ideal" woman becomes angry only when other people's needs are at stake—her child's safety, her husband's reputation. Her own needs don't merit such a fuss.

Many women, sensitive to this cultural prohibition, identify their own anger as pathological. "What's wrong with me? Other people don't seem to get so bothered. How can I be a good mother (or wife, or employee, or parishioner) and be so angry? I must be sick." And frightened to find themselves angry, women typically work hard to dispel the feelings. "Things are not really that bad," a woman tries to assure herself. "Besides, there's really nothing that can be done to change the situation. And it's probably all my fault anyway."

Therapists describe another pattern some women use to deflect their anger. Psychologist Robert Mark notes that "many women go right from sadness to forgiveness, skipping anger completely. And the reason they skip anger is because they're afraid of abandonment." Girls, growing up with the cultural message that masculinity is potent and preferred, often learn that women can't make it on their own. To survive in this kind of world, the cultural scenario continues, women must be connected with and protected by men. Not surprisingly, then, many women have understood themselves and their value in terms of their connections with other people, especially men. A woman alone is unwanted, unacceptable. Worse, she is unprotected and at risk. For a woman like this, anger is dangerous.

Psychologist Dana Crowley Jack shows how many married women experience anger's risk. "When a woman is furious with her partner for his affairs, or his emotional unresponsiveness, or his threats to leave, she may be afraid that if she makes her feelings known he will retaliate with even greater anger or by acting on his threats to leave." Caught in this double bind, "a woman can feel that any action she takes carries the threat of loss." A woman convinced that she cannot make it on her own will judge anger her enemy. She can let herself feel hurt and sadness, because these emotions threaten her connections less. They may even help win over her partner, if guilt and pity induce him to change his behavior. But anger's assertive claims remain out of bounds.

Ashamed of their anger (because it is unfeminine) and afraid of its consequences (because it risks upsetting powerful people or disrupting significant relationships), many women feel trapped. They can neither acknowledge their anger as valid nor can they use its energy to improve a bad situation. But suppressing their feelings doesn't make the bad situation go away. Instead, the cycle of anger/inaction/frustration repeats. In some women, the consequence is a deepening sense of helplessness and inferiority: "I am angry all the time, but there is nothing I can do to make my life better. I am just a victim here."

Other women develop a pattern of occasional angry outbursts. Blowing up every once in a while sometimes helps, at least in the short run. Letting off steam gets other people's attention. Physically, the tantrum releases some of her pent-up frustration; often a sense of vindication temporarily boosts her self-esteem. But most women report these angry outbursts make them feel worse in the long run. Looking back, a woman recognizes her angry response was exaggerated—sparked more by accumulated grievances than by the single event that triggered the flare-up. This tends to leave the people who witnessed her angry display confused about the issues really involved. Often she is herself confused! And the angry blowup seldom works as an effective strategy for change; the people targeted in such an attack defend themselves and respond in kind. And most women, finally, feel embarrassed and guilty about this public display of their distress. So they apologize, undercutting their anger's validity instead of following through with a clear call for change.

Men and Anger

Conventional gender rules warp men's experience of anger, too. In U.S. society, aggression—a willingness to do harm to someone else—is widely accepted as a necessary, even enviable, trait of real masculinity. Professional football and hockey ritually celebrate the rites of manly aggression. And most men learn early on to equate anger with aggressive behavior. The Stone Center researchers trace the pattern of socialization that teaches boys this lesson.

Most boys learn anger's rules from their fathers, who feel charged with the responsibility to "make a man" out of their sons. Fathers want to equip their sons to succeed, or at least to survive, in a society they themselves know to be brutally competitive, frequently unfair, and unforgiving of weakness in any form. To get ahead, a man must be tough. So the father's job is to toughen up his boy.

How is this to be done? Many American fathers adopt a strategy of making their sons angry, then channeling this arousal into aggressive behavior. Studies of parents regularly report that fathers play more rough-and-tumble with their sons, almost from birth, than with their daughters. A father's physical roughness usually escalates as the little boy grows up. What was previously a father's playful punch feels to his son now like a blow meant to cause pain. Corporal punishment often increases, becoming the father's customary way of disciplining his son. In some homes, emotional harassment increases as well. Many men recall childhood experiences of their father's berating them in public, calling them belittling names, holding them to impossible standards of achievement, and mocking them if they failed. And these are fathers who love their sons! Their intent is not to harm but to do what is best for their boys, preparing them to take up the demanding tasks of masculinity.

Whatever the father's intent, a son's expectable response to this kind of treatment is anger. But the boy's expression of anger toward his father is blocked. Early on, he lacks the resources to fight back and he senses that his weakness itself is shameful. And besides, he is told— and often knows for himself—that his father loves him, in spite of this hurtful behavior. What happens to his angry arousal? Fathers prod their sons to focus this urgency in another direction. Boys learn to use their anger to compete, to contest, to win out over others, to best the opponent—all skills required to make it in a man's world. By adolescence, most young men have learned well to translate their angry arousal into combative behavior.

This induction into "masculinity" complicates anger for men. First, the little boy learns to disown his feelings of anger, since anger toward an all-powerful father is unacceptable, even dangerous. And anger seldom comes alone. In the face of his father's bullying behavior, the son experiences a host of unpleasant feelings—hurt, confusion, fear, frustration, and more. Especially, the child feels vulnerable. Denying his anger usually results in turning away from these other threatening emotions, too. The boy learns to separate himself from *all* these feelings, not just anger. If this early pattern of disconnecting from his feelings goes unchallenged, the boy reaches manhood emotionally off-balance. Unsure what he is feeling, his inner world remains alien: well-hidden from himself and unavailable to those close to him.

Second, the little boy learns to connect feeling vulnerable with acting aggressively. The script for masculinity instructs men to deflect angry arousal into aggressive behavior. And these links between arousal and aggression are forged early, before the little boy can sort out the feelings that frighten him. Along with distress at his father's harsh behavior, for example, the boy senses himself to be weak, undefended, exposed. Feelings of anger and vulnerability become intertwined. But boys in our culture realize quickly that feeling vulnerable is not only frightening; it is incompatible with being a real man. As they learn to deny angry feelings and deflect this energy into manly aggression, most boys learn to respond to their feelings of vulnerability the same way. Many men continue this pattern as adults, responding combatively in situations where they feel weak or vulnerable.

Luise Eichenbaum and Susie Orbach describe a pattern of response they see frequently in their clinical practice: "a man gets very frightened when he sees that the woman is upset or angry with him. He may try to protect himself and defend against his own vulnerability. He may feel like a little boy being told he has disappointed or upset his mother. He may not know how to give or what to give. Often men's vulnerability and feelings of inadequacy are converted into anger. The anger operates as a defense to cover up the vulnerable feelings and protect them from exposure." Social analysts suggest that these culturally ingrained links between vulnerability and aggression help explain the epidemic of violence against women in our society.

The Angry Woman's Journey

We may also examine woman's anger through the prism of social change. In a provocative analysis of changing black consciousness, psychologist James Fowler discussed an expectable process of cognitive transformation experienced by African Americans whose lives were influenced by the civil rights movement. In our own work, we have used Fowler's analysis to explore how people's experience of anger shifts with their involvement in the broader dynamics of social change.

These shifts describe a pattern shared by many groups struggling against ingrained prejudices to craft a positive social identity—new immigrants to this country, persons challenged by physical handicaps, gay men and lesbians, lay people in the church. We will focus here on the role of anger in the changing social consciousness of women.

Conventional Thinking

When they first confront the women's movement, many women are at the stage of conventional thinking. Conventional thinking accepts society's definitions as accurate; reality equals the *status quo*. In conventional thinking, cultural norms shape our own experience; the way we understand ourselves fits how society wants us to be. We hold ourselves accountable to living the way society says we *should*, convinced that's the right way. When our thoughts or behavior deviate from what is expected, we feel guilty. Instead of questioning whether the roles and rules make sense, we blame ourselves.

At this stage, women's thinking is dominated by what psychologist Ellen McGrath calls the *Traditional Core*. "The Traditional Core is a woman's cultural conscience, a core of traditional values and thinking that exists deep within every woman and dictates how we must behave and what roles are 'right' and 'wrong' for us to fulfill." The Traditional Core's list of roles and behaviors appropriate for women includes many positive elements—nurturance, receptivity, unselfishness, patience, willingness to express emotion, concern for relationships. Society needs these deeply human qualities, and most women cherish these qualities in themselves.

But McGrath and her research associates found that many women carry the Traditional Core not as a commitment to personal values but as a debilitating set of rules. For some women, the weight of these cultural expectations becomes suffocating.

At the stage of conventional thinking, a woman accepts the social rules that are in place. When she runs into the limits of the woman's role, she may be disappointed but she seldom senses that injustice has been done. "This is just the way things are; I might as well make the best of it."

In conventional thinking, we model our lives on these rules. And if the rules don't fit—if they work against our growth or constrain our

Ten Commandments of the Negative Traditional Core

I. Thou shalt take care of thyself only after taking care of all others.

II. Thou shalt not take the name of men in vain.

III. Thou shalt not threaten abandonment no matter how bad it gets.

IV. Thou shalt be seen (and thou better look good!) and not heard.

V. Thou shalt be economically and emotionally dependent on men.

VI. Thou shalt always be thin.

VII. Thou shalt never grow old.

VIII. Thou shalt service men sexually whenever they wish.

IX. Thou shalt never consider thy work more important than a man's.

X. Thou shalt not assume any rights beyond what men have bestowed on thee.

— Ellen McGrath, *When Feeling Bad Is Good*

creativity—we judge ourselves, not the rules, to be deficient. "Perhaps if I tried harder I could finally get it right. Why can't I be more generous? I should give these rules another chance; surely other people know better than I do!" And if the extra effort still doesn't bring success, our likely response is not anger but guilt. Even knowing we are not directly at fault, we still feel somehow to blame for falling short of the image of a "good woman."

So, the Traditional Core holds anger hostage. Even when they recognize their circumstances are bad, women at this stage are often reluctant to assert themselves. Or they let grievances accumulate until their rage explodes, usually with little useful effect. In either case, anger is unavailable as a resource.

Dichotomous Thinking

But more and more women have come to a new awareness of themselves, beyond the rigid gender definitions they once accepted. A woman's movement beyond conventional thinking is often gradual. Slowly she recognizes that her own experience of being a woman doesn't fit the way things are supposed to be. Margaret talks about her own transformation.

> I was trying so hard to be the woman everybody wanted me to be— my parents wanted me to be married soon, my boyfriend wanted me to be more supportive of his career, my boss wanted me to be grateful, while he took credit for much of my work! I was trying to lose weight, to dress for success, and to act demurely so I wouldn't threaten my male associates. I remember I came home from work one evening, closed the door in my apartment, and shouted out loud to the empty room, "This doesn't make any sense!"

At first Margaret, like many women, thought that she must be the problem and tried to change herself to fit in again. But as the conflict between personal hopes and outside demands intensified, Margaret's focus shifted. "I realized that the main problem isn't me but some crazy set of rules I'm trying to live by. But the rules don't work, at least not for me. Who made them up, anyway?"

Confronting the discrepancy between her own experience and the culture's definition of her proper role marks a turning point for a woman. Her life has given the lie to the claims of conventional thinking. She may feel she has been misled, even betrayed. No longer docile in the face of culture's demands, a woman begins to disbelieve.

Change begins here. As social analyst Elizabeth Janeway reminds us, to initiate change we must disbelieve that the way things are is the way things have to be. If we cannot question the status quo, we remain powerless to alter it. But questioning the status quo isn't easy. Trusting our own experience is difficult when it contradicts what most people seem to accept. Sometimes our new awareness contradicts even what we used to accept as normal and necessary. Early in disbelief we are tempted, like Margaret, to think, "If I'm the only one who sees things differently, maybe I'm the one who's wrong. Perhaps it's just my problem." And the status quo has much to gain from keeping the problem personal. As long as a woman's distress is a private matter, there is no cause for political alarm. Personal solutions are sufficient. She can take a vacation or take a pill, join a health club or see a therapist. The powers that be may even come to her aid, offering resources to help her fit in once again. It is not altruism alone that motivates this institutional generosity. A savvy power structure knows that therapy is always cheaper than social change. A woman spending considerable energy dealing with "her problem" is unlikely to bother the political arrangement. Underlying definitions remain unchallenged; current structures remain in place.

Disbelieving culture's demands leaves a woman with the task of developing new criteria for living in the world. Cultural guidelines that once served her are now suspect. But as yet no reliable alternatives have emerged from her own still-barely-trusted experience. In this vacuum, the criteria of *dichotomous thinking* emerge. In dichotomous thinking we simplify the world, perceiving reality in terms of stark opposites: good and bad, friend and enemy, female and male. The scales have fallen from our eyes! Now conscious of the hidden faces of discrimination, we are suspicious of motives and gestures and behavior that previously were of little concern. We see male chauvinism everywhere—in part because it is so widespread, in part because of our new sensitivity.

Being at the dichotomous stage is difficult, difficult for women and difficult for other people in their lives. Women here feel considerable anger: against the culture that has lied to us, against the norms that continue to constrain us, and often against the men among whom we live and work. Much of the anger that a woman at this stage experiences is justified; she has to contend with sexism daily. But a woman in the dichotomous stage often experiences anger that goes beyond the evidence. New awareness of the ways that women have been—and can still be—abused changes her perception of things. The conventions of social life—a married woman using her husband's last name, women in the military being excluded from combat duty, even seeing men opening doors for women or picking up the restaurant check—infuriate her, even if she's not directly involved.

To some observers (and to women in this stage as well!), a woman's anger at the dichotomous stage may seem exaggerated and unfocused, but her rage is not without value. For many women, anger is an important spur to moving beyond conventional thinking. Standing against the accepted norms and conventions of one's culture is not easy; pressures mount, some from within: "I'm not being a good girl. People won't like me if I start making demands." Many from outside, as spouses and children urge us to act like we used to and church and civic authorities warn us of dire social consequences of our unnatural complaints. Where does a woman get the strength to side with her own still-fragile new awareness, against the weight of prevailing cultural norms? Some of the strength comes from our anger.

"My anger has meant pain to me but it has also meant survival," poet Audre Lorde attests, "and before I give it up I'm going to be sure that there is something at least as powerful to replace it on the road to clarity." In anger we feel powerful physically. Anger's judgment of injury received helps us remain convinced of the legitimacy of our concerns—"we are many and our cause is just." Anger reminds us of the hurts we have suffered. Being angry keeps us from backsliding, from returning to the earlier easier patterns that were killing us but at least didn't make other people mad.

But granting that our diffuse public anger can be useful, living through this angry stage is seldom easy. A woman finds herself angry much of the time; people nearby are offended and potential allies feel rebuked. Let's acknowledge first that not everyone moves beyond dichotomous thinking quickly. For some women, the sharp distinctions of dichotomous thinking continue to describe, and circumscribe, their experience. The clear categories of right and wrong continue to separate "our kind" from "those others," women (or at least the women who agree with us) from men. But many women report another important movement in self-understanding, with an accompanying shift in how they embrace their anger as part of social transformation.

Integrated Thinking

We can speak of this shift as a movement toward *integrated thinking*. Making this move doesn't mean leaving our anger behind. Women have lots to be angry about! The realities of sexism continue to shape women's lives. In the face of such injustice, anger is appropriate. But a woman's anger at this stage is more seasoned, more open to her decision and control. Carol Tavris reports the shift she observed in women active in the feminist movement: "At first anger is indiscriminate, the prism through which all experience is refracted; slowly, anger becomes selective." A woman colleague describes her own experience.

> I'm really in a different place now. Last year I think I was angry all the time. There's still lots to be angry about! And I'm still often furious at the inequity and discrimination all around. But much of

it doesn't seem like malice to me now—a lot of the injustice I run into comes from people's selfishness and just their ignorance. That doesn't make their actions right, of course. But seeing this bigger picture helps me decide how to be angry and when, sometimes, just to let it go.

In the dichotomous stage, women sometimes feel overwhelmed by anger. As we move toward integrated thinking, anger continues as a frequent companion but less as a tyrant. A participant in one of our workshops used this helpful image. "My anger used to be in the driver's seat. Now we've changed places. I'm glad my anger is close at hand. I need it in the back seat to keep me going, but now I'm the one doing the driving." Here our anger is accompanied by choice. Another woman offered this testimony to the change, "Now when I'm angry I can be more objective. I can take time to evaluate my feelings, to determine what triggered the anger and what direction my response should go. I can decide whether—and how—to express the anger I feel."

This stage is *integrative*, helping a woman incorporate her anger into her awareness as a responsible self. The stage allows for social integration as well. When we are in the dichotomous stage, many women identify all men as "the enemy." We sense that some action or inaction on their part is responsible for the injustices that women experience. And this perception is often accurate. But in dichotomous thinking, this "them against us" attitude dominates to such an extent that it overwhelms evidence to the contrary. All "them" are suspect; their support is discounted as patronizing, their critique is dismissed as typical male animosity. At the integrative stage, a woman's judgments become more nuanced. Yes, some men are hostile and demeaning and antagonistic toward women. But men are numbered among our friends and supporters as well. We can acknowledge those men who have called us to life and celebrate those who have championed women's cause. We come to appreciate that the line that divides good and evil does not neatly separate women from men. Rather it cuts through the heart of each person, even ourself.

With integrated thinking, a woman can acknowledge her own ambivalence and appreciate her collusion in her own oppression. She wants to be accepted as a responsible adult and treated as a person in charge of her own life. But leaving the really difficult decisions to others is tempting, especially when that strategy avoids the messy possibility of making a mistake on her own. She resents being treated as a sex object, but a little flirting now and then sure is fun.

Integrated anger is a genuine accomplishment, especially for many of us who have learned that expressing anger is unladylike and even dangerous. Anger becomes part of our moral response. "The moral use of anger," Carol Tavris concludes, "requires an awareness of choice and an embrace of reason. It is knowing when to become angry—'this is wrong, this I will protest'—and when to make peace; when to take action, and when to keep silent; knowing the likely cause of one's anger and not berating the blameless." Seeing anger as an acceptable part of herself, a woman comes into possession of an important resource for continuing her commitment to both self-protection and social change.

Reflective Exercise

Recall a time recently when your *angry feelings* were troublesome for you. Spend some time with this memory, taking notes to bring the experience vividly to mind. Then list for yourself the factors that made this experience troublesome: factors in you, factors in the situation.

Then recall a recent time when *expressing anger* was difficult for you. Again, list for yourself the factors that made the experience difficult for you: factors in you, factors in the situation.

If possible, share this reflection with a friend or discuss your experience in a group that includes both men and women. Note the similarities and differences that emerge. Do the differences seem to be gender related? Are other factors more significant—age, education, economic status, ethnic origin? What does this discussion suggest to you about the culture's rules for anger?

Additional Resources

Psychologist Carol Tavris provides a comprehensive and readable review of current research findings in *Anger—The Misunderstood Emotion*. In chapter 7, she examines "Which Sex has the Anger Problem?"; we quote material from pp. 49, 185, 273, and 285. Tavris expands the discussion of research findings on gender differences in *The Mismeasure of Woman.* William Frost and James Averill report their work in "Differences between Men and Women in the Everyday Experience of Anger." Sandra Thompson's *Women and Anger* makes available the initial findings of an important ongoing research project at the Center for Nursing Research of the University of Tennessee.

Jean Baker Miller and her colleagues at the Stone Center of Wellesley College continue their critical contribution to the understanding of psychological issues affecting women's lives. Miller's analysis of "The Construction of Anger in Women and Men" sets the parameters for much of the subsequent discussion. See also Teresa Bernardez, "Women and Anger—Cultural Prohibitions" and Jean Baker Miller and Janet Surrey, "Revisioning Women's Anger—The Personal and the Global."

Audre Lorde's testimony to anger's role appears in her essay "The Uses of Anger: Women Responding to Racism." Ellen McGrath's discussion of the Traditional Core is found in *When Feeling Bad Is Good;* we quote from pp. 53–55. For James Fowler's early analysis of changing African-American consciousness, see his essay "Faith, Liberation and Human Development." Carolyn Osiek exemplifies the resilience of integrated anger in *Beyond Anger: On Being a Feminist in the Church.*

Anne Campbell updates the ongoing discussion of cultural influences on personal behavior in *Men, Women, and Aggression.* For additional perspective on current gender research, see Deborah Tannen, *You Just Don't Understand: Women and Men in Conversation* and Ellyn Kaschak, *Engendered Lives: A New Psychology of Women's Experience.*

Therapist Robert Mark's comments appeared in Barbara Sullivan's article "Temper, Temper" in the *Chicago Tribune* (June 27, 1990). Harriet Goldhor Lerner identifies both cultural and intrapsychic factors in "Internal Prohibitions against Female Anger," found in her book *Women in Therapy.* In *Understanding Women: A Feminist Psychoanalytic Approach,* Luise Eichenbaum and Susie Orbach draw on both theory and clinical practice for a provocative examination of anger in relationships between women and men; we quote from p. 189.

6

How We Deal with Our Anger

*Any damn fool can have rage. What takes guts is
to take the anger and rage and do something with it.*
Salvador Villaseñor

V ictor Villaseñor is the author of *Rain of Gold*, an epic account of
an extended family—his own—in Mexico and the United States
over several generations. His work has won critical acclaim for its
elegant style, meticulous research, and univeral sympathies. Recently
Villaseñor spoke of his own growing up in southern California in the
1940s and '50s. The son of Mexican parents, Villaseñor felt the full
weight of the cultural message: Mexicans are not as good as other
people. At nineteen he spent a year in his parents' homeland. There
he came in touch for the first time with his own heritage. Villaseñor
was startled to see government officials, professional people, teachers,
artists—all persons of color who looked and spoke like him. Though he
was severely dyslexic throughout his years in U.S. schools, in Mexico
Villaseñor met a woman who taught him to read, opening him at last
to the world of books. This exhilirating exposure to Mexican culture
and literature nourished his confidence. As pride in his Hispanic roots
surged, Villaseñor felt growing anger over his early experience in the
United States. "I had so much rage and anger, I didn't want to come
back to the United States." Villaseñor recalls a crucial conversation
he had with his father at that time. "If I come back, I might want to
kill," the son declared. "You don't think I have rage?" the senior Villaseñor retorted. "Any damn fool can have rage. What takes guts is to
take the anger and rage and do something with it."

How do we deal with our anger? As Victor Villaseñor's father knew,
giving free range to rage seldom helps. An angry outburst may momen-

tarily vindicate our sense of honor, but at heavy cost. We come away from the fray with people injured, relationships wounded, potential allies alienated. Regret cannot undo the harm done when anger turns to assault, whether in family life or in random social violence.

Most of us know from personal experience other responses that don't work: *denial* (I'm NOT angry!), *guilt* (I'm angry, but I shouldn't be), *self-condemnation* (What right do I have to be angry, since whatever is wrong is probably my fault), or *blame* (No, it's YOUR fault I'm angry). These reactions doom anger from the outset.

Dealing effectively with anger demands a different starting point: we might name it acceptance but "acceptance" sounds so patronizing. The benefits—and risks—of anger inspire more than reluctant assent or begrudging tolerance. How do we *befriend* our anger? First, we honor it, then we evaluate it, then we tap its energy to help us act positively for change.

Honoring Anger

Anger is always ugly, but it doesn't
always have to be bad.
Hendrie Weisinger

Honor captures the *awe* and *respect* that anger provokes: "Here is a formidable, even dangerous, emotion." Anger threatens the delicate web of social life. Unattended, its energy erodes relationships and risks degenerating into vengeance. But access to this energy is indispensable.

In the dictionary, *to honor* means both to recognize and to respect. How do we honor anger? Recognizing that angry feelings are normal is a good place to start. Honoring helps us hold this formidable emotion as expectable, inevitable, allowable in our life—without rushing into actions we will later regret. Simply acknowledging "Yes, I feel angry" begins to release us from the burden of denial. The esteem implied in the word *honor* serves as an antidote for the wounded attitudes that many of us carry still, especially a tendency to punish ourselves for feeling angry. Instead of being beseiged by guilt over an outlawed emotion, we learn we can accept our anger even as we struggle to decide what to do about it. Reaffirming for ourselves the difference between *feeling* angry and *acting* enraged takes us a long way in taming anger's power.

Anger signals "passion ahead; proceed with caution." Honoring anger helps respect this power. To honor anger we have to pay attention to what we are feeling. The effort of paying attention counteracts an impulse to respond too quickly. This discipline interrupts the urgency of our arousal, giving us time to consider consequences. Psychological studies show how paying attention helps people respond well to anger. Summarizing more than a decade of research on how people deal with their emotions, psychologist Leonard Berkowitz describes a pattern of reflection found among people who are able to regulate negative moods effectively. Berkowitz discovered that paying attention starts a significant process of discernment. When people first become aware of their anger, for example, "they are somewhat surprised or disturbed and this prompts a relatively high level of cognitive activity. They think about the possible causes of their feelings and even consider what may be the best way to act. These considerations then steer their behavior." When attentiveness does not intervene, Berkowitz found that "the hostile and aggressive tendencies created by the negative mood are less likely to be restrained and are likely to be expressed openly" in harsh language and violent actions. A commitment to honor anger encourages us to pay attention to our feelings. And paying attention helps us read anger properly and use its power productively.

Evaluating Our Anger

Anger's always been hard for me to deal with. Some of my friends call me a hot-head; I admit I'm likely to respond immediately if I feel slighted or if somebody takes advantage of me. And sometimes that's good, but sometimes not. Lately I've been getting a better hold on my anger. Something that works for me now: when I start feeling angry, I say to myself "My anger is trying to tell me something." I keep repeating the phrase, like a mantra. This calms me down, but also points me in the new direction. Instead of flying off the handle, I try to look more closely at what's making me mad . . . and why. And that's been a real revelation to me!

"My anger is trying to tell me something." Anger always carries information, but its message is seldom immediately clear. Befriending anger includes finding ways to retrieve this message. The first step is to interrupt our typical pattern of response. For some of us the automatic response is finding a scape-goat, someone to sacrifice to our rage.

Searching out a culprit shields us from facing our own part in the problem. This stance warps anger's strength for self-defense into a strategy of self-delusion.

Or our customary response may be to give in when we are angry. Perhaps we've learned that anger is terribly unladylike, or seriously sinful, or patently immature. Or we may fear the consequences of our own or other people's rage. So we acquiesce, hoping that refusing to assert ourself will make the feelings go away. "I don't want to upset anybody; it's dangerous to demand my rights; protesting would be impolite." This compliant stance, too, subverts the revelation our anger may hold.

Sandra Thomas, director of the Anger Research Project at the University of Tennessee, recommends a simple strategy to help uncover our automatic response. "Keep a log of your anger experiences, recording with whom you become angry, to whom you express it, to whom you do not express it, how long it lasts, and what thoughts accompany it." Soon patterns will emerge, giving us a better sense of what our own anger looks like. Evaluating these patterns helps us decide what we want to do differently.

"My anger is trying to tell me something." In befriending anger, the response to be nurtured is readiness to learn. To learn what? Something about ourself: the risks we sense to our self-esteem. Or the ways our personal histories have left us vulnerable to hurt. Or how events and circumstances trigger this vulnerability into rage. Since anger erupts when deeply held convictions are threatened, being angry can reveal the values we hold worth fighting for. Tracking our anger back to its source can also uncover a rift between our professed values and how we are really living. Anger here is an ally of our integrity, challenging us to make the changes necessary to get back on course.

Or anger may be trying to tell us something about our world. Being angry is a response to frustration. For many of us, the frustration is lack of time: our irritability stems from a sense that we're falling behind. We strain against the seemingly endless demands of workplace and family responsibilities. For others, anger reveals the weight of other people's expectations. We live in a world where many people feel they have a right to dictate to us, setting goals we should achieve and faulting us for failing standards that are not our own. Our frustration may point to a troubled relationship: a valued colleague undermines our authority in public; a teenage son retreats into silence or verbal abuse. Or anger alerts us to a significant setting become dangerous: a climate of racial intimidation pervades our neighborhood; the threat of sexual harassment erodes our confidence at work. Examined, our anger can give insight into how our environment has become hostile and start to show us the shape of an effective response.

"My anger is trying to tell me something." Discerning this message requires effort. We stop to reflect on what triggers our angry feelings; we interrupt a customary pattern of response to ask what needs to be questioned or challenged or set aside. Evaluating our anger inserts a pause in our arousal, leaving space for anger's wisdom to emerge.

Discern the Appropriate Response

Determining how to act with anger starts by focusing on our goal: what do we want to accomplish here? Sometimes the goal is communication; we want to let someone know how we feel. Sometimes the goal is change; we want to remedy a bad situation. And sometimes the goal is conversion; we want to turn away from our anger and move on. Each of these options involves decision.

Seeing angry behavior simply as a spontaneous eruption beyond our control is misleading, because angry action always involves choice. Being angry is better understood as an interpersonal strategy, one of the ways we learn to deal with other people. For example, people decide *whether* to show their anger, *how* to express it, and *who* will be its focus—whether a spouse or a pet or a stranger on the street. Befriending anger means learning how to make the choices that transform our arousal into effective response.

Many of us learned early that "feeling angry is bad," a lesson that limited our choices to denial and repression. But when refusing anger's arousal deprived us of its energy, we recognized our composure came at too high a price. For us the chief discipline is to carry our arousal forward into effective action.

But in many American families, children learn different lessons about anger. Early on the links between anger and violence are reinforced: by parents who, when they are angry, discipline their children by harsh physical punishment; by adults who characteristically handle frustration by lashing out; by violent arguments and assaults in the home. If this is our early experience, befriending means breaking the pattern that automatically links angry arousal to violent behavior.

Experimental programs are being developed in schools and rehabilitative centers and elsewhere to help violence-prone young people learn ways to break these links. From what has been learned so far, three strategies seem key. First, teaching young people simple ways to interrupt their anger—deep breathing, relaxing stretches, counting to ten, using their imagination to take them somewhere else. Second, showing young people how to find alternatives to their explosive response by introducing them to basic conflict-management skills—considering different ways to communicate their anger, learning nonviolent ways to be assertive, tracking the consequences of their actions. Third, helping young people find support for new ways of acting—setting up peer groups committed to change, encouraging them to identify people and situations to avoid, establishing adult contact persons to whom they can regularly report both their successes and mistakes. Obviously, troubled children are not the only ones who might benefit from these helpful strategies.

Expressing Anger

In close relationships, letting the person who has upset us know of our distress often helps. Rochelle Albin notes that "expressing anger not only provides relief for ourselves, it can also help other people see things differently. Expressing anger relieves hurt and can change things." In fact, Beverly Harrison insists, "anger expressed directly is a mode of taking the other person seriously." When anger arises, Harrison continues, "we have two basic options . . . We can ignore, avoid, condemn, or blame. Or we can act to alter relationships toward reciprocity, beginning a real process of hearing and speaking to each other."

Telling a friend or coworker how her action offends us may not be easy, but—if skillfully done—this honesty makes change possible. Our friend may not have meant to hurt us; she may not even have known we took offense. Aware now how her behavior affects us, she can take steps to act differently.

Communicating anger sometimes leads to more than changed behavior. Where people care for one another and for their life together, expressing anger can deepen intimacy. Letting someone know our distress opens our inner world to them. Anger exposes us, revealing where we feel vulnerable. Telling someone how they have hurt us risks giving them information that can hurt us more. But in a safe relationship, revealing our vulnerability—paradoxically—strengthens us. Having been angry with one another, and survived through that sweaty distress, strengthens the relationship as well.

Sadly, not all close relationships are safe, and not every angry statement supports positive change. Sometimes expressing anger just makes things worse. Carol Tavris cautions that, contrary to some common sense recommendations, "letting it all out" usually increases our rage. Anger dissipates when injustice is rectified, when a sense of personal control is reinstated, when self-esteem is restored. Giving vent to angry feelings can sometimes be part of this process, moving us beyond apathy and prompting us to get involved. But "getting it out of our system" usually does not dissipate hostility; on the contrary, angry expression tends to increase anger—in ourselves and in other people.

Psychologist Ron Richardson observes that many angry people act on the supposition "if I just show how upset I am, the other person will change." He warns that angry expression makes a clumsy tool for change. Since people under seige strike back, verbal attack is usually counterproductive. But expressing anger does not demand hostile behavior. We can let someone know that we are angry and why, without attacking them verbally or physically. To show the difference, therapists distinguish between a communication style that starts with information about oneself ("this is how I am feeling now . . . ; this is what I am going to do . . .") and messages that insult or blame the other person ("it's your fault, stupid!; Look what you have done to me . . ."). In situations where emotions run high, "I" messages often make it easier to give and receive information. When our goal is to move beyond anger—toward understanding, toward negotiation, toward peace—these communication skills become crucial.

Acting with Our Anger

Anger moves us to remedy a grievance. Sometimes expressing anger is enough and just letting people know our complaint brings the change we need. But most often the world doesn't come around quickly in the face of our displeasure. We have to do more than register our distress; we have to strategize how to effect change. When our goal is change, the challenge is channeling anger into effective action.

Acting *with* anger means holding our anger in a new way. Rather than moving away from our arousal, we want to stay in touch with its urgency. In the face of entrenched bias or long-term patterns of abuse, change can seem impossible. Falling back into a resigned stance that "nothing can be done" or "it's not my job to make thing better" is tempting then. Resistance seems worthless. But giving in to this sense of futility saps our strength. Losing touch with our anger, we fall out of the loop of social transformation.

When apathy threatens, we need disciplines to keep our anger alive. Anger has a dangerous memory, since it commits us to action. By holding in mind the injustice we have witnessed, by recalling injuries we have received, by remembering our worth, we rouse ourselves to act.

But sustaining anger is risky to do by ourself. Remembering anger also rekindles emotional pain. Fear of facing that force alone makes us reluctant to stir anger's ashes. Better, perhaps, to turn away from the evidence of personal malice or social inequity and get by as best we can. Finding support, then, can be one of the disciplines of anger. With companions who share our anger, we gain a sense of power that goes beyond what we can do alone. By providing a setting in which our distress can be acknowledged and then focused into action, a supportive group also protects us from simply being overwhelmed by the arousal we feel. The group helps us hold our pain so that we can draw on its energy to act.

When our goal is to remedy a bad situation, anger gives us steam to make things change. But being steamed up doesn't guarantee success. Channeling anger into effective action is the real work of change. Strategies of planning and problem solving are key—being clear about what we want to accomplish, recognizing the barriers we face, gathering needed resources, enlisting allies to help. But anger remains an underlying energy of social transformation, fueling personal commitment and sustaining social resolve.

Cold Anger

The community organization movement shows how personal anger contributes to social change. Mary Beth Rogers followed the work of Ernesto Cortez and his associates in the Industrial Areas Foundation. Committed to grass-roots community organization in the tradition of political activist Saul Alinsky, IAF's goal is revitalizing democracy through active citizen participation. Its basic strategy is nurturing leaders within poor and working-class communities, leaders who then support their community's efforts to identify its needs and engage the local political structure in meeting these needs. Cortez himself worked closely with the development of Communities Organized for Public Service (COPS) in the Mexican-American neighborhoods of San Antonio. His experience there, as in other IAF projects in New York, California and Texas, convinced Cortez that a common energy motivates the most effective local organizers—personal anger.

The emotion Cortez looks for in leaders is not violent rage or hostile resentment but "cold anger," a disciplined impulse rooted deep in personal experience. "Most people feel uneasy with the prospect of using their anger, so they suppress it or deny it, only to have it appear hot and uncontrollable in inappropriate times and places," Rogers remarks. "Cortez works with the leaders he develops to get them to remember their personal anger, to understand its sources, and then to draw on it as fuel for the energy they need to confront those who hold power over their lives."

Cortez believes that social change happens when the injustices we suffer personally become a bridge connecting us with other people's pain. This shared pain, held collectively, transforms complaint into compassion. And compassion tempers our self-destructive wrath, forging cold anger as a potent resource that sustains commitment. To show this dynamic in action, Cortez turns to the story of Moses leading the Hebrews out of slavery in Egypt: "The memory of their oppression is so strong it is like a burning bush, a fire that never goes out, an unquenchable fire. That memory is powerful, has a force of its own. It's hallowed ground. That's what we mean by anger."

Letting Go Anger

Acting *with* anger can be an appropriate, even virtuous response. But often enough we need to turn away from wrath. When recalling a grievance spirals us into despair, our goal is to move beyond anger. When rage provokes us to respond recklessly, our goal is to dissipate its force. Later reclaiming this energy may be useful, but now it needs moderation.

Since we experience anger in both mind and body, both mind and body can help us let go. Moderate physical exercise—taking a walk, gardening, even doing laundry or cleaning house—channels energy away from angry behavior. Spending time in yoga or meditation lowers the body's physiological arousal, lessening the physical sense of urgency. Getting involved in activities that demand concentration and give us pleasure—such as pursuing a favorite hobby or preparing a festive meal—helps bring our body around and calm our emotions as well. And when we are angry, doing something generous for someone else almost always transforms our mood. Anger harbors the impulse to punish other people; helping people counteracts that urge. Hostility drains away, even when the recipient of our good deed is not the person who has angered us.

Reappraisal is another useful strategy for lessening anger's hold. A change in interpretation can be as effective in dislodging anger as a change in our bodily state. For example: our anger at being kept waiting dissolves when we find that our tardy companion had a compelling reason. Or we excuse an apparent insult when we recognize the strain under which the other person is living now. Learning of new facts or extenuating circumstances helps us put our displeasure in wider perspective. Often this wider view diminishes our anger.

Laughter, too, helps us put anger aside. Humor reinterprets the meaning of events, setting our frustrations and failures at a new angle. Humor gives us perspective, helping us view differently the provocations that make us mad. And being able to laugh at ourselves lessens the impact of the assaults and reversals that are inevitably part of living. Taking ourselves less seriously lets us see through some of the petulant demands we make of life. So most of the time, laughter heals anger. But humor is a tricky tool. Laughter can trivialize as well as relativize. And many of us have felt the force of humor used against us, in efforts to make us feel foolish for our anger or to belittle our concern.

Forgiveness in Anger

Forgiveness, too, reinterprets anger. And it can be the gift of anger courageously faced. Forgiveness allows us to start again, to come to a sense of a new beginning. In forgiving we *choose* not to let the hurt we have experienced get in the way of a relationship continuing. The common sense adage is "forgive and forget." And for most of us, experience confirms that our efforts to forgive are helped by being able to forget. Yet forgiving is not the same thing as forgetting. Forgiveness knows that hurt has been sustained. But in forgiving we respond to the other person not in terms of the harm they have inflicted but in terms of who they are beyond that pain. So the order of the adage is important: forgive . . . and then forget, lest the memory of the pain revive the anger and hostility between us. Social philosopher Hannah Arendt notes that "forgiving is an eminently personal (though not necessarily individual or private) affair in which *what* was done is forgiven for the sake of *who* did it."

Forgiving involves a decision, but it is not completed in the moment of choice. Forgiveness is a process that gradually allows hurt to heal as trust rebuilds. The process of forgiving does not bring us back to where we were, allowing us to go on as if nothing has happened. Something *has* happened, something profound. The fabric of our interwoven lives has been torn. Yet we can choose not to be defined by this rupture, incorporating it instead as part of an ongoing relationship. We hope the hurt will not become the pattern, but we sense its contribution of depth and substance to the design.

Forgiveness is not easy to extend or to receive. To forgive, we must face the offense and experience our pain. We have to test our anger to see if these feelings are justified. Submitting our anger to this kind of scrutiny, we may find that we have misjudged another's motives or overreacted to an event. Our commitment to being angry may tempt us to nurse our indignation and refuse to acknowledge our mistake.

The reflection forgiveness requires often shows us ways we have contributed to the problem. In few situations is one person solely to blame. Most interactions are conjoint, with each of us part of the painful pattern that develops. But sometimes casting ourselves as the innocent victim seems safer than risking the self-knowledge that forgiveness demands.

Genuine forgiveness also robs us of our hurt; we can no longer harbor it for later use against the person to blame. Instead, we must surrender the wound that has become a cherished, if bitter, possession. By letting this hurt go, we lose the painful advantage we had been savoring but we regain the energy we have squandered in nurturing our vengeance. Forgiveness evens the score, undercutting the sense that we have something to hold over others. In forgiving, we start out anew, perhaps humbled (we know how fragile our relationship can be) but hopeful too.

If offering forgiveness is hard, receiving forgiveness can be more difficult. To accept forgiveness, we must revisit the harm we have done, acknowledging our responsibility or admitting our mistake. Asking forgiveness humbles us, so denial tempts us to resist. As long as we are in the right, we need seek no pardon. To accept forgiveness is to confess our guilt—not only to another but to ourself.

Times exist when forgiveness is not our goal, or at least not the goal right now—situations in which the demands of justice or change take precedence over the restoration of a relationship. These are seasons when anger needs to be sustained, not set aside. But when reconciliation is the goal, forgiveness is a powerful ally. Often it is the only door to peace.

Sometimes, it seems we cannot talk enough or explain enough or regret enough to move beyond anger. The harm has been too heavy, the distance between us now seems too broad to be bridged. These times teach us that forgiveness is more than personal achievement. We learn again its power often comes as gift—a grace that, spent by our anger, we must await in hope.

Reflective Exercise

Consider your own experience in dealing with anger. Bring to mind a time you handled your anger well. First recall the circumstances: the setting, the persons involved, what triggered your anger, how you responded, the way things turned out.

Now spend some time with these questions: What did you like about the way you dealt with anger here? As you see things, what was most useful, productive, helpful? Then, what did you dislike about the way you dealt with anger here? Looking back now on that experience, what would you want to do differently?

Finally, what convictions do you bring from your own experience to add to the chapter's suggestions for dealing with anger?

Additional Resources

Victor Villaseñor's discussion of anger with his father is quoted by Jorge Casuso in "Epic in the Making," *Chicago Tribune*, December 5, 1991;

for a fuller acccount of Villaseñor's compelling family history, see his book *Rain of Gold*.

Gary Hankins and Carol Hankins explore effective ways to deal with anger in *Prescription for Anger: Coping with Angry Feelings and Angry People*. Sandra Thomas's suggestions for practical ways to learn from our anger appear in Jane Brody's "Personal Health" column in the *New York Times*, November 24, 1993. Ron Richardson recommends simple strategies for effective expression of emotions in *Family Ties That Bind*. See also *Facing the Fire: Experiencing and Expressing Anger Appropriately* by John Lee and Bill Stott; *Fighting Fair: A Non-Violent Strategy for Resolving Everyday Conflicts* by Mark Juergensmeyer; and Hendrie Weisinger's *Anger Workout Book*.

Leonard Berkowitz discusses research findings that underscore the importance of paying attention to our anger in "On the Formation and Regulation of Anger and Aggression"; we quote from p. 501. Rochelle Albin's comment on expressing anger is from p. 83 of her book *Emotions*; Beverly Harrison's comment is from p. 15 of her essay "The Place of Anger in the Works of Love."

In *Cold Anger: A Story of Faith and Power Politics*, Mary Beth Rogers introduces the people and principles of the Industrial Areas Foundation grass-roots community organization effort; we quote from pp. 190–91. Charles Curran examines the contribution of community organizations to the moral tradition of social transformation in "Saul D. Alinsky, Catholic Social Practice, and Catholic Theory."

Doris Donnelly gives graceful assistance to the tasks of personal and social reconciliation in *Putting Forgiveness into Practice*. David Schell writes engagingly about the challenge of genuine forgiveness in *Getting Bitter or Getting Better: Choosing Forgiveness for Your Own Good*. See also Lewis Smedes's helpful discussion in *Forgive and Forget: Healing the Hurts We Don't Deserve*.

Part Three

SHAME AND GUILT—
THE PRICE
OF BELONGING

The Chinese character for shame (ch'ih)
shows a heart next to an ear:
the blush that reveals embarrassment or humiliation

7

The Boundaries of Belonging

The *Iliad* is Homer's classic account of the Greek triumph at Troy. In the central action, Achilles kills Hector in battle. His rage unsatisfied even by this bloody victory, the hero drags Hector's corpse behind his chariot around the walls of Troy. This dishonorable act—defiling the body of a defeated enemy—offends friend and foe alike. Outraged by his cruelty, even the gods are provoked to denounce Achilles: "He has no shame—that gift that hinders mortals, but helps them too."

At heart, shame and guilt are benefits—"gifts that hinder mortals but help them too." Humans have an insatiable desire to be part of the group. We long to belong. We yearn to be chosen and to be included, sensing our very survival is at stake. Left alone, without the safety and nourishment of companionship, we are doomed. Shame and guilt are social dynamics monitoring our lifelong efforts to belong. Often working together, these painful emotions guard our social identity by warning us of personal transgressions that threaten to exclude us from "our kind."

The Journey from Shame to Guilt

Shame takes center stage in the first act of the human drama of belonging. For the ancient Greeks, shame was a social conscience, a warning that a person was trespassing a community agreement. In this same season of human history, the sages of Hebrew Scripture evoked shame repeatedly as a powerful guardian of their people's bond with God: "O My God, I am too ashamed and embarrassed to lift my face to you, my God, for our iniquities have risen higher than our heads . . ." (Ezra 9:6). In China, Confucius linked virtue and proper conduct with this same emotion: "If you are led by virtue and conform to proper conduct, you will have a sense of shame and be good" (Analects II, No. 3).

Several centuries later, just before the time of Christ, the social consciousness of shame began to be accompanied by a deepening sense of personal responsibility—and its companion emotion, guilt. The concept of guilt was not unknown before this, but earlier the word referred predominantly to a legal judgment of wrongdoing; a person was *found* guilty by others. Gradually guilt came to describe a conviction of fault rendered by an interior judge. In this sense, guilt arises as a personal awareness of our own failings.

In our own lives, each of us recapitulates this cultural journey from shame to guilt. Moral philosopher Sidney Callahan recalls the dilemma parents face: "Children must be kept safe, be trained to be acceptable to the larger society, and be encouraged to flourish as unique persons. These goals . . . can be accomplished only when reluctant children are persuaded to do things they do not wish to do." At first persuasion comes from the outside, as parents and other caregivers enforce the rules of belonging—"this is how you must behave here." As children learn how to fit into family and neighborhood and society, they gradually internalize these once-external values as their own. Now when we fall short of what is expected, we don't need others to remind us. We have moved from disappointing others to disappointing ourselves! Ambiguous as such a transition seems, we must remember this development is an advance. We now carry our culture's ideals as our own. The best values of our family and faith and nation survive as we accept and internalize them. No longer acting simply to please others and avoid shame, we act out of personal responsibility and conscience. We have moved from shame to guilt.

The interior governor of guilt does not simply replace the social arbiter of shame; instead guilt joins shame as another guide to our belonging. While both emotions are, by nature, troublesome, they remain resources we cannot do without. But injury to these interior resources easily throws us off stride. Then we carry constant concern about pleasing other people, worried that they might disapprove of us. Or we fret over whether we have ever done enough, afraid that we have somehow shirked our duty. These wounds twist shame and guilt, designed as guardians of our belonging, into tyrants. In chapter 9 we will continue our examination of guilt; we turn now to the complex emotion of shame.

Shame as Grace and Disgrace

Nicholas was glad it was raining. He would be able to wear the yellow boots and matching rain hat that he had received last week for his birthday. Throughout the school day he kept a close check on the boots that stood out like beacons among the drab raingear in the coatroom.

But on the way home after school, disaster struck. Nearly home— only two blocks to go—he was stopped by three junior high boys who started to make fun of his boots. They grabbed his rain hat and knocked open his book bag, spilling the contents. Nicholas himself slipped and fell on a muddy patch of lawn. Confused and frightened, he began to cry, evoking the older boys' mocking laughter. Kicking his hat into the mud, they ran off in search of other prey.

Nicholas gathered up his books and hat and trudged home. When he entered the house his eyes were red and he choked back tearful sobs. Sizing up the situation, his mother held him in a long embrace and then helped him off with his muddy clothes. "Are you okay, Nick? Can you tell me what happened?" Hearing her small son's tale of woe, she sympathized with his fright and humiliation: "Those big boys ganged up on you! That's terrible. You must have been really scared. I'm so glad you are all right now."

When his father come home later, Nicholas got to tell his story again and receive more solace. Then his parents spoke with Nicholas about what could be done to prevent his being frightened like that in the future. Perhaps he could walk to school and back with his older sister for the next few weeks. His parents could call the principal to see if other children had been victimized. Nicholas might change his route home to pass along streets where the school traffic guards were more in evidence. That last plan sounded best to Nicholas, and his parents agreed. Feeling battered but cared for, he went to bed early that night.

Across town a similar scene is played out. Terry, on his way home from second grade, runs into older bullies blocking his path. Here too the older boys terrorize the frightened younger one, dumping out the contents of his backpack and pushing him to the ground. Terry's tears draw the boys' scorn; they run away hurling shouts of "Big baby!"

Like Nicholas, Terry slowly gets up and begins the trek home. As he walks Terry recalls a recent family event. He hears his parents scolding an older brother who had been involved in a neighborhood fight: "Why did you let those kids push you around? You're old enough to fight back. No son of mine should let himself be treated that way. We don't take that stuff from anybody. And stop that whimpering! What are you, a sissy?"

Now added to Terry's fright and humiliation is a painful realization: his feelings of confusion and embarrassment are unacceptable to his parents. This belittling incident should not have happened to him. More significantly, he should not have these feelings. Now Terry is ashamed of feeling ashamed. So he resolves to remain silent about his unfortunate encounter with the bullies. Nobody needs to know.

Exposed at the Boundary

Shame is about exposure. To be exposed, as Carl Schneider reminds us, means to be "out of position." The leader of a holiday parade or religious procession is suddenly embarrassed. Walking too fast, she has gotten "out of position" and stands exposed: out of step with the rest of the group. Most of us feel exposed when we stand out in a crowd— we seem too heavy or too dark-skinned to be found attractive, too poor or too assertive to be welcome here. Other social situations leave us feeling oddly exposed. A person dining alone in a restaurant feels a bit uncomfortable. Since eating is such a communal act, we sense ourselves slightly "exposed" or vulnerable when we eat alone in public. And at the scene of a death, we cover the corpse; leaving the deceased person exposed to casual view strikes us as somehow disrespectful. The English word *shame* shares the same root with the word *chemise*—a shirt or slip that covers us. With us as with Adam and Eve in the garden, the experience of shame is one of exposure and our immediate response is to cover ourselves, even to hide.

"Shame supposes that one is completely exposed and conscious of being looked at . . . one is visible and not ready to be visible." These words of psychologist Erik Erikson catch the ambiguity of our social existence; we want to be seen, to be acknowledged and respected.

But only when we are ready, only when we feel adequate to stand in another's gaze.

In adolescence we feel this ambivalence with a special poignancy. We desperately wish to be recognized, to be known and accepted for who we are. But we are petrified of being exposed. Our changing bodies, becoming more adult and more sexual, make us visible in new ways—whether we are ready or not. Sensing how vulnerable we are to other people's appraisal, we hesitate to reveal ourselves. "Not yet," our embarrassment cautions. Not until we can change our clothes or change our opinions or change our friends—so that we finally get it right.

In adolescence and well beyond, embarrassment is an ordinary part of our social life. Regularly we find ourselves too close, too exposed, too vulnerable in our interactions with one another. At these critical and often painful moments, shame serves as a healthy warning system. By acknowledging this emotion and trying to understanding what has triggered our distress, we can learn lessons important for our life. In chapter 8 we will explore these benefits that healthy shame brings. But shame does not always come bearing gifts.

Recall the two young boys we met earlier. Nicholas's family responds to his shame with attention, empathy, and grace. By acknowledging his confusion, they honor his pain. Their practical respect for his humiliation begins its healing.

But Terry's experience is different. Anticipating how his parents will respond, Terry feels his embarrassment as disgrace. So he tries to bury the experience, hiding it from others and if possible from himself. But hidden from consciousness, unattended, this ordinary feeling of shame—his appropriate response to being belittled—begins to fester. When this pattern becomes a regular response, a healthy sense of shame deteriorates into a truly negative emotion—a debilitating feeling that poisons his life.

Nicholas's parents block his descent into destructive shame by acknowledging that the pain he feels is appropriate. He learns that this dreadful feeling—humiliation—is not a sign of his inferiority. Nicholas is as strong and capable as he should be at this age. The bigger boys took advantage of him; they, not Nicholas, are in the wrong here.

Terry, enveloped by a less healthy environment, senses that his feelings of shame signal his own inadequacy. If he were smarter or better or tougher, he guesses, maybe he would not have to feel like this. And he has no one to tell him otherwise. Knowing no other way to deal with this distress, he pushes the painful feelings away. What he takes from the experience is strong motivation to do whatever it takes to avoid feeling like this again.

The Perils of Childhood

As children we lack the strength to resist the intrusions of adults; parents and others are able to do with us as they will. Robert Bly describes what can occur.

> If a grown-up moves to hit a child, or stuff food into the child's mouth, there is no defense—it happens. If the grown-up decides to shout, and penetrate the child's auditory boundaries by sheer violence, it happens. Most parents invade the child's territory whenever they wish, and the child, trying to maintain his mood by crying, is simply carried away, mood included.

Bly shows how this vulnerability leaves children susceptible to a deeper shame.

> Each child lives deep inside his or her own psychic house, or soul castle, and the child deserves the right of sovereignty inside that house. Whenever a parent ignores the child's sovereignty, and invades, the child feels not only anger, but shame. The child concludes that if it has no sovereignty, it must be worthless. Shame is the name we give to the sense that we are unworthy and inadequate as human beings.

Being imposed on as children—whether physically, psychologically, or sexually—throws us off balance. Unable to resist the interference of powerful people, we sense this intrusion is an indictment of our own worth. Acutely aware that others can cross our boundaries at will, we find trusting ourselves difficult. The healthy response of shame, bruised this early, turns toxic.

Children growing up in such a hostile setting are likely to respond in one of two ways. Some of us learn that we have no defendable boundaries. Other people come and go as they will, without regard for our person or privacy. Intimidated by their power, our only hope is to please and placate these intruders. If we cannot escape their presence, perhaps at least we can avoid some of the painful feelings. Growing up, we may become very adept in these "people pleasing" tactics. We seek out a service career—ministry, health care, counseling. Or we marry a partner we can care for full time. Our selfless behavior looks virtuous to us and other people, at least until we recognize its compulsive force. Then comes a stark confrontation with the underlying shame that propels so much of what we do.

A second reaction to early wounds is to build boundaries that cannot be trespassed. Acutely aware of our fragility, we erect barriers to protect ourselves. Gaining weight may be our defense. For boys, a weight gain often signals physical power. Working out in the gym, practicing martial arts, developing muscular strength means "nobody can take advantage of me now." But weight has a different symbolic meaning for girls. Our culture equates beauty with being slim; it condemns heavy women as unattractive. A young woman wounded by shame may gain weight to protect herself. In her experience, people coming close means threat. Fat, she hopes, she will be safe—even if alone. A colleague, the veteran of a fourteen-year struggle with an eating disorder, describes the strategy: "A shamed person eats compulsively to wrap herself in a layer of fat that will be a protection against letting anyone in to see her true self."

Such stout defenses have to influence our spiritual life. A workshop participant shared with us the influence of sexual abuse on her relationship with God. "My experience of the presence of God has always been pain. God is one who violently breaks through my protective shields." A deeply religious person, she found prayer increasingly difficult. Whenever she would start to feel God's closeness as consolation, she found herself blocking that awareness by "rebuilding the walls protecting myself-of-shame, retreating back into my worthlessness from a God whose very being proclaims worth." Puzzled by her strong ambivalence, she came to recognize that for her, "every connection is a violation. I am ashamed to be connected." Realizing the threat that close contact held for her and acknowledging the "peril" of a God whose very presence announced her worth, she was gradually able to move to a new stage of healing.

An Unspeakable Emotion

In our ordinary bouts of embarrassment, we are tempted to cover ourselves, to hide. More traumatic experiences of shame render us mute. Physical and sexual abuse in childhood can leave us speechless; we have no words for this assault and its pain remains too raw to acknowledge out loud. This terrible feeling sinks into our soul as a paralyzing silence. Adult survivors of incest often report that they did not know their sense of worthlessness had a name; they just assumed this is how bad it feels to be alive.

In this way what begins as a social emotion—an alarm of shame generated in interaction with others—becomes privatized. But shame suppressed does not stay silent. Instead shame recruits other emotions to speak for it.

A person may feel constantly afraid. All close contact threatens her; every conversation could exposure her inadequacy; any interaction might end with the other person taking unfair advantage of her. Such fear no longer serves its healthy warning function, alerting a person to real dangers. Instead she is anxious all the time. Enlisted by the hidden emotion of shame, her fear now stands on constant alert. Why she is so afraid confuses her. What she does know is that feelings of unworthiness erupt frequently, flooding her with pain. What causes these dreaded feelings remains hidden to her, so her attempts to confront them are seldom successful. What she is left with is her familiar fear that the painful feelings will return. But persistent fear makes a costly survival strategy. To placate her anxieties, she shrinks from life. Overcaution tempts her to avoid all risks, to hold all relationships suspect. Better to remain on guard, lest the fragile boundaries of her self-esteem be breached again.

In another person shame recruits the emotion of anger. A middle-aged man is constantly upset and irascible, easily provoked with no apparent cause. His silent shame finds daily but disguised release in bitter, hostile behavior. In this man's life, anger acts not merely as a hedge against humiliation but as a wall to block all advances that might expose him to others or provoke his self-contempt. Here anger loses its healthy purpose: no longer an emergency response, its arousal has been enlisted in the full-time service of shame. This, too, is a strategy of survival. But it takes its toll in damaged health and injured relationships.

Sometimes shame speaks through compulsive achievement. Self-doubt contaminates the confidence of the child who is constantly told "what you've done is not good enough." Bringing home a report card with four As and one B elicits a parent's disappointed rebuke, "I know you can do better than that." A young pitcher allows only one run to score in the little league baseball game. His competitive father forgets to praise this accomplishment, urging him instead to try harder: "Concentrate when you're up there on the mound! Next time you should make it a no-hitter." Sensing that he has disappointed his parent, the boy intensely feels his inadequacy. Ashamed of himself, he vows to try harder. But how much is enough?

A child like this often brings to adult life an impressive drive to succeed. But even when success comes, he can seldom rejoice in his achievements. The inner critic is never satisfied: "you could do better next time!" As he pushes himself harder, pleasure and gratitude drain from his life. His energy for over-achievement is rooted ultimately in a profound sense of unworthiness, another name for shame.

In his award-winning book *A Bright Shining Lie*, Neil Sheehan tells the story of John Paul Vann, one of the most decorated heroes of the Vietnam war. Vann's bravery in combat impressed all who knew him. He defied danger, apparently unconcerned for his own safety or the odds against a mission's success. In addition, his energy seemed endless: on assignment Vann regularly worked two 8-hour shifts every day over long stretches of time.

Sheehan's chilling account of Vann's early life gradually uncovers the links between his public valor and private shame. Growing up in a severely troubled family, Vann used daring to hide a deep-seated fear of inadequacy. His reckless courage and relentless vigor masked the shame that fueled his life, and finally brought him to his "heroic" death in a helicopter crash in Vietnam.

Healing Shame

Destructive shame hides in secrecy and silence. For healing to come, we have to bring our pain to light. As John Bradshaw observes, "We have to move from our misery and embrace our pain. We have to feel as bad as we really feel."

Many of us have begun this journey. Long hesitant, we finally bring our torment to a friend or counselor, hoping their wisdom will salve the pain. What we discover is that the simple act of saying our distress starts to diminish its hold on us. The pain does not automatically go away, but now it serves more as a stimulus to change than simply as self-punishment.

The healing starts within. Therapists Marilyn Mason and Merle Fossum describe their efforts to help clients recognize shame as a *learned* response. The profound sense of inferiority they carry is not a realistic assessment of their worth, but an interpretation they learned in a damaging environment. As adults, they can set aside these crippling self-definitions and learn to value themselves anew.

Other therapists use metaphors to describe the healing process. Being severely wounded by shame is like living in a room with many doors, but all the doorknobs are on the outside. Others enter our room as they will; we have no say, no warning, no defense. The goal of the difficult struggle to acknowledge our shame and trace its origins is to return the doorknobs to their rightful position on the inside of the doors. Then we can determine who enters our world. Intimacy becomes safer, since we can decide who and when and how to be close. Sharing and self-disclosure are possible, even welcome, since we no longer see ourselves as simply victims.

Carl Schneider reminds us that healthy shame is about self-awareness. This emotion focuses our gaze on ourself, inviting a sometimes painful—sometimes mellow—recognition of our limits and vulnerabilities. Like healthy guilt, the painful proddings of shame can deliver us from distorted ideals and the compulsions that feed on them. The bruising insight of shame sees through the props and deceptions, the roles and arrangements we have used to disguise ourselves even to ourselves. Healed, shame helps show us who we are. John Bradshaw describes this grace:

> The healing of the shame that binds you is a revelatory experience.
> Because your shame exists at the very core of your being, when
> you embrace your shame, you begin to discover who you really are.
> Shame both hides and reveals our truest self.

The healing of shame returns us to ourselves: limited, fragile, real. We are delivered from a desperate need to please others and the other addictions that had covered up and numbed the pain that had no name. More comfortable with our limited self, we discover that others are not simply the enemy. And we are eager again to belong.

Reflective Exercise

Adolescence is a season of embarrassment for most of us. Return in imagination to your own high school years. Spend some time remembering where you lived at that time and with whom, who your friends were at school and elsewhere, the activities and events that filled your days.

Now, recall a time when you felt ashamed as a teenager, an experience of being painfully embarrassed. For example, you may have felt embarrassed about your body, or ashamed of your family, or your religious or ethnic background. Once you have remembered a particular occasion, stay with that memory for a while, trying to recall the circumstances that evoked your embarrassment. Be mindful, too, of the range of other feelings that came along with shame here.

As you look back now on that experience, how did you deal with the shame or embarrassment? How successful were your efforts then? Do you sense any connections between that adolescent experience and your life these days?

Additional Resources

Helen Merrill Lynd's early work, *On Shame and the Search for Identity*, stands as a foundation of today's psychological interest in this issue. For a readable overview of current psychological consensus, see Robert Karen's article "Shame" in The Atlantic Monthly (February 1992). In *Shame: The Power of Caring*, Gershen Kaufman carefully traces the movement of shame from an interpersonal experience to a toxic interior mood; Kaufman also provides insight into the connection of shame with other painful emotions such as anger and depression.

Carl Schneider explores the significance of exposure on p. 34 in *Shame, Exposure and Privacy*; see pp. 25–28 for his discussion of shame and self-awareness. Erik Erikson's definition of shame appears in his classic work, *Identity and the Life Cycle*, p. 71; see also his restatement of this theme in *The Life Cycle Completed—A Review*. Sidney Callahan discusses the parents' dilemma in her essay "Does Gender Make a Difference in Moral Decision Making?"; we quote from p. 75.

Family therapists Merle Fossum and Marilyn Mason explore the dynamics of shame in the cycle of control and addiction in dysfunctional families in *Facing Shame*. In *Uncovering Shame*, clinicians James Harper and Margaret Hoopes encourage a therapeutic approach that integrates individuals and their family systems. Carl Goldberg's *Understanding Shame* offers a guide to clinical treatment for persons debilitated by early experiences of shame; see also Ronald Potter-Efron and Patricia

Potter-Efron, *Letting Go of Shame.* John Bradshaw gives an excellent, readable overview of the toxicity of shame in *Healing the Shame That Binds You;* see p. 237 for the passage quoted in this chapter.

Robert Bly discusses the potency of shame in the young child in his *Iron John*, p. 147. *A Bright Shining Lie*, Neil Sheehan's Pulitzer Prize-winning book, is based on his earlier *New Yorker* article examining the life of Vietnam war hero John Paul Vann.

8

Healthy Shame: Will and Warrior

> We can remove our clothes, without removing our sense of shame.
>
> *Plutarch*

The emotion of shame embraces a bewildering range of feelings: the momentary embarrassment when we notice that the zipper on our pants or skirt is open; the deeper humiliation of losing our job and feeling like a public failure; the profound shame that still binds us three decades after an experience of sexual abuse.

Shame's status among the negative emotions is well-earned. The threatening exposure of our vulnerability wounds us in many ways. How could shame be anything but a curse? How can these feelings of worthlessness connect with anything helpful? To heal this negative emotion we must recover our sense of shame as a positive and healthy sensitivity.

More Than an Emotion

Shame is about being seen. We long to be recognized, to be held in respect. We also fear being seen: what if we are judged inadequate? What if others see through us? What if, like Nicholas and Terry, we are discovered in our weakness? Shame names the sharp sense of humiliation that public exposure brings.

But the word *shame* refers to more than bitter feelings of embarrassment. Shame also names the inner attunement we bring to our encounters with other people. This sense of shame is the healthy sensitivity we feel as we come close to others. A gradually developed disposition, this positive resource alerts us to the vulnerable boundaries that both link us to and separate us from one another. When this sensitivity is violated, the painful feelings we call shame result.

Even these painful feelings serve as a positive guide to our belonging. A healthy sense of shame is the impulse of discretion that makes us hesitate as we draw close to another person. Is this someone we can trust? Should we risk telling her about a concern that deeply troubles us? A sense of shame is the healthy apprehension we feel when we ask a friend about his recent divorce: Is this the right time? Or are we intruding on his privacy? Our sense of shame generates the ordinary anxiety we feel as we weigh sharing something personal with a colleague: Is revealing ourself to this person appropriate? Is it safe?

Healthy shame is about tact: literally, how to be in touch. Tact is the ability to gauge how close to come to another, when to look away, when to allow extra space between us. Tact is the uncanny resource that allows us to draw close while leaving each other's integrity intact. Tact helps us develop strategies for approaching others and techniques of disclosing our heart without doing harm. These tactics may, of course, become mere tools of manipulation or attack. But in their best guise, tactics serve the imperative of intimacy.

A healthy sense of shame acts as a gyroscope, helping us keep our balance amid the dizzying challenges of social life. It guides our approaches and helps us make mid-flight corrections. We appreciate this resource when we recall a common pitfall of many social occasions. A casual acquaintance approaches us at a party and starts to discuss some intimate details of his private life. Instantly an internal distress signal sounds: "This conversation doesn't fit!" Suitable, perhaps, with a psychological therapist or pastoral minister or close friend, here his disclosure is out of bounds. He has come too close; his revelation tells us more than is appropriate for us to know. Our palpable discomfort responds to this boundary violation, alerting us to protect ourself from his intrusion.

Composure

The little boy peeks out from behind his mother's skirt, then disappears. Again, he hazards a quick look, giggles and returns to his safe hiding place. Who can resist the fascination of this game? As the child both hides and reveals himself, he gains our attention and recruits our affection.

Shyness is one of the charming dynamics of a healthy sense of shame, even among adults. A person holds back as we draw close. She hesitates or blushes. As the person retreats, we are drawn toward her; frequently we find this demurral to be attractive. This hesitance charms us and mysteriously charges the space between us with excitement. The author Milan Kundera describes the special allure of shyness:

> He had known her for a year now, but she would still get shy in front of him. He enjoyed her moments of shyness, partly because they distinguished her from the women he'd met before, partly because the girl's shyness was a precious thing to him.

But this natural shyness can become distorted and turn into a false modesty. A person may learn to be *too* hesitant, *too* apprehensive as he approaches the boundaries that connect him with others. If a healthy sense of shame attunes us to the real limits of our self, a false modesty makes us overly conscious of our fragility. What begins as modesty becomes a wall that seals us off from all threatening contact with others.

British psychologist Adam Phillips, in his enchanting book *On Kissing, Tickling and Being Bored*, discusses this damaging withdrawal as *composure*. Infants have no composure—and need none. Oblivious of boundaries, the nursing baby assumes the breast is but an extension of her own body. But as the child comes to recognize the difference and distance between self and others, developing composure—"a calculated social poise"—becomes necessary.

As adults, composure is something we frequently regain rather than permanently possess. Recoiling from our over-exposure to an emotional stimulus, we try to recover some quiet and control—to restore our composure. But we can become too good at this mode of "self-holding and self-protecting." Retreating from contact, we hold ourselves too aloof for too long. This withdrawal tactic generates "an appearance of self-possession" that communicates "a relative absence of neediness." But such rigid composure transforms our self-holding into self-hiding which, in its extreme form, "insulates the individual from ever allowing the recognition he seeks."

Phillips suggests that composure, this holding ourselves apart from others, may be linked to one of our deepest aspirations. More than simply an exercise of self-defense, composure may be "a kind of self-holding that keeps open the possibility of finding an environment in which the composure itself could be relinquished." Perhaps our best hope is to "create or find an environment in which [our] composure was of no use, and in which this fact was no longer a problem." As a strategy of healthy shame, composure protects our vulnerable boundaries. But, like shame, composure hopes for recognition. We long for the place and persons where our composure will no longer be necessary, where we might be, in the words of Genesis, "naked and unashamed."

An Erotic Sensibility

A healthy sense of shame guards the boundaries of our bodily self. And many of us experience the painful feelings of shame most powerfully in our bodies and our sexuality. Here we sense the fragile frontiers of our necessary and perilous exchanges with other people. Recall the excruciating embarrassment of the teenager taking off her clothes for a medical examination. In a season of high vulnerability, the young person feels the danger of exposing a body that is newly sexually charged. But even in acute experiences like this, shame remains a social instinct: others help us be more comfortable with our sensitivity. The professional respect with which the nurse or doctor uncovers our body teaches us important lessons. Without being embarrassed or embarrassing us, they model a finely honed sense of modesty.

Moral philosopher Bernard Williams reminds us that the Greek word for positive shame, *aidos*, is connected to the word for genitals. Literally, then, this emotion concerns our erotic life. Classical Latin employed the phrase *pars pudenda*—often translated as "private parts"—to designate the genitals. The different emotional nuances that are attached to *pars pudenda* illustrate our ambivalence about sexuality. A translation influenced by the Greek language renders the phrase as that "vulnerable part" of the body that deserves special respect; a translation more influenced by certain strands of Christian piety renders the phrase as our "shameful parts"—parts that are considered unholy, even disgusting.

At the time the gospels were being compiled within the early communities of Jesus' followers, the Roman author Plutarch spoke eloquently of shame as an erotic virtue: "We can remove our clothes, without removing our sense of shame." Yet in both the Septuagint version of the Hebrew Bible and in the New Testament the Greek word for healthy shame is virtually absent. In its stead, we find the virtue of respect (*timē*), sometimes used with explicitly erotic overtones. In his first letter to the Christians in Corinth, St. Paul twice links this virtue to our bodiliness. "You were bought for a price [*timē*]; therefore glorify God in your bodies . . . (1 Cor. 6:20). Our worth is rooted in God's having saved us, and the mutual respect this calls for must be registered in our bodies.

In chapter 12, Paul evokes the imagery of the community of faith as the body of Christ. Like a physical body, a Christian gathering is composed of a variety of members, each blessed with unique gifts and wounded by injury. Our integrity as a group of believers depends on the respect we have for each other, whatever our position in the body. Paul alerts his listeners to be especially sensitive to the weaker members: "those members of the body that we think less honorable we clothe with greater honor; and our less respectable members are treated with greater respect. . . . God has so arranged the body, giving the greater honor to the inferior member" (1 Cor. 12:23, 24). "Inferior member" echoes the erotic *pars pudenda* of every physical body, and the care and respect these vulnerable members deserve. Paul's metaphor about the body Christian alerts us to the "vulnerable members" of the social community today—the ill and the immigrant, the homeless and the sexually marginalized. The community of faith is charged to give special respect to these "less honorable members" of the body politic, to whom—Paul insists—"God has given the greater honor." We fail as a Christian body when we disrespect the vulnerable members of the human community, when our own behavior simply mimics the culture's condemnation and neglect.

Shame and the Development of Will

Healthy shame stimulates the development of personal will. Will is the capacity for sustained and self-directed activity: this inner strength is rooted in our confidence in who we are and finds expression in our determination to live out our personal convictions. To show how shame supports personal will we return to an early season of development, "the terrible twos."

As two-year-olds, children move beyond the all-encompassing dependence of infancy. Newly developed skeletal strength means we can stand and walk on our own. Muscular advances increase our capacity to control urination and defecation. And parents are eager to teach us how to use these newfound abilities. Now that we have the strength to get away, they are intent that we learn what we can and cannot "get away with." So instruction intensifies: what to eat, where to relax our sphincters, when to bathe, how to dress ourselves. In all these ways our caregivers are showing us how to belong, how to act so that we fit in this society.

As two-year-olds learn the lessons of belonging, they also awaken to the possibility of "no." The growing child now has strength not only to walk, but to walk away—to escape parents' full control. She can resist potty training or refuse to eat some strange-looking food. In these unavoidable early battles between parent and child, the struggle between belonging and autonomy is joined. The child must eat and eliminate and dress according to its group's dictates; but the child recognizes that she must also be herself. Saying "no" lays down the gauntlet to the formation of the "ideal child"—a perfect reproduction of the parents' desires. In this early resistance, personal will is forged. And shame is the catalyst.

As parents struggle to shape the toddler's social behavior, they recognize that rational persuasion has its limits. The small child still lacks the cognitive ability to trace cause and effect, to see links between action and consequence, to weigh the merits of various choices. A more direct approach is demanded. Parents typically resort to shaming techniques to enforce their desires on their child. Cajoling ("Be a big boy!"), name-calling ("You're just a crybaby"), and threats of punishment and abandonment compel the child to act as expected, to behave as instructed.

Shame is the bad feeling that arises when children realize they have done something that significant people find improper. Even if we did it unknowingly (the parent discovers the child exploring his penis), even if the action was beyond our control (wetting the bed), what we have done is held against us. The distressing feeling of shame gets our attention. It signals that we have failed in other people's eyes; we have fallen short of their expectations. And these bad feelings provoke a new movement in the child's maturity.

The sting of shame confronts the child with the cost of acceptance: "this is what you must do to belong." Caught in the tension between belonging and autonomy, the toddler struggles to develop, in the words of psychologist Erik Erikson, "a sense of *self-control without loss of self-esteem.*" Without this tension between self-control and social compliance, the child's development is stunted. Only in the struggle do we learn how to resolve inner desires with outer demands. Shame acts as an irritant, stimulating us to fight back. And from the resulting conflict, Erikson reminds us, "a lasting sense of autonomy and pride" may emerge.

If the force of shame overwhelms, the child may capitulate and simply conform. He then sets out on a course to always please, never offend, to fit in perfectly, making his parents proud of him. This shame-bound behavior puts him in lifelong jeopardy; always alert to what will please others, he abandons interior criteria of what is right for him. In the developmental schema of Erik Erikson, self-doubt swamps autonomy. Personal will, the root of an individual's sense of identity and purpose, fails its first developmental test.

But being damaged by shame early can produce the opposite reaction. The child rejects the demands of others and sets out on an overly autonomous journey. Insistent on doing it his way, such a person rejects convention and compromise. Obsessed with independence, the person develops a fierce determination to avoid any external influence. Severely irritated by shame, such a child seeks too much autonomy.

Healthy shame directs both conformity and resistance. In the "no's" of the two-year-old we see the first fruits of this stirring of independence. In this perilous season of balancing the "yes" to our parents' demands and the "no" of our own will, we begin the journey to self-confidence and self-esteem. Gradually finding the balance between conformity and independence, we come to a sense of our uniqueness, our peculiar identity and calling in life. This personal confidence strengthens us in the face of social pressure and institutional shaming. It provides us with the daring to risk new ventures that have not been approved or sanctioned by social authorities. The interior strength of will equips us with the resilience even to fail at such efforts, without being too ashamed and without having a particular failing mushroom into a judgment that we are a failure.

Shame is a dangerous dynamic in the process of socialization. This powerful emotion, if abused by those who are teaching us how to belong, may destroy our confidence and defeat the development of will. But, when it is blended with affection and tolerance in early childhood, shame impels the toddler to craft a balance between belonging and autonomy. Through this important contribution, shame becomes a disguised gift on the journey toward adult maturity.

Shame and the Development of the Warrior

In their influential discussion of cultural archetypes, Robert Moore and Douglas Gillette retrieve the ancient image of the warrior. This mythic figure embodies the energy that emboldens us to face danger and test the limits of achievement. Admittedly, the metaphor seems tainted today. For most of us, "warrior" conjures up the rattle of swords. Even using the image risks justifying the trademark violence of conventional masculinity. Does our culture's aggression really need encouragement? But Moore and Gillette argue that the accurate portrait of the warrior is as one who protects the boundaries, more defender than aggressor. This concern for boundaries hints that the warrior is also an ally of positive shame.

The warrior stands at the origins of our determination and courage. While Moore and Gillette explore this image in men's experience, its fierceness is not exclusively a man's trait. The single mother who struggles to raise her children in the midst of poverty must have the fierceness of the warrior. The woman who pursues a vision beyond the conventional roles of marriage and motherhood will need the determination of the warrior to succeed.

As a Jungian archetype, the warrior embodies the impulse to set out on risky journeys. This impulse originates as the *hero*—a daring youthful enthusiasm that is still ignorant of its own limits. Eager for achievement, the hero in us courts adventure and challenge. Our buoyant bravery, still immature, is undaunted by personal danger and unconcerned for other people's sensibilities.

As maturity teaches its painful lessons of personal limitation, the hero dies. In its stead emerges the warrior, now disciplining our native fierceness with a wisdom born of experience. Conscious of our limits, the warrior in us acts as a wise tactician, deploying our courage for the battles that count.

When the warrior in us has been wounded, we can't summon the proper fierceness for self-defense. Fear of conflict saps our determination, our desire to please leaves us vulnerable. We shrink, becoming passive and accommodating, reduced to the status of victims. Or, early injury spurs the warrior to aggressive overcompensation. We are driven in our work, where compulsive purpose cloaks our shame and tries to cover our sense of inadequacy. In relationships we throw up impregnable boundaries. The goal: No one will get near our heart; no one will come close enough to hurt us again.

The warrior defends the necessary boundaries—in relationships that bring us close to others, in circumstances when we must say "no." Positive shame stands at the boundaries, too, helping us discern how close to come and how soon and with whom. The dual resources of will and warrior prove indispensable in adult life, transforming simple enthusiasm and abandon into tested steady resolve.

The Virtues of Shame

Shame is more than a momentary embarrassment or a destructive mood of inferiority. As a positive resource, it embodies the crucial strengths of will and warrior. With proper care, a positive sense of shame matures into a resident strength in us—a virtue. Bernard Williams, a moral philosopher and classics scholar, describes the development of the virtue of shame in Greece in the fifth century before the common era. During this period the Greeks distinguished between a servile shame that simply pivoted on public opinion and a healthy shame rooted in personal conviction.

In its most robust dimension, a sense of shame affords a person "a sense of who one is and what one hopes to be." If guilt concerns what we have done, shame concerns who we are. Guilt addresses correctness, but shame addresses worth.

For Williams, shame's virtuousness depends on the internalized *other* whose gaze evaluates our actions. This "other" may embody only our parents' authoritative frown on our childish endeavors. But it may also mature into conscience, when our best inherited values, rather than tyrannical authority, serve us as interior guide. As Sidney Callahan observes in her study of conscience's role:

> In our internalized memory, we can carry our inner, unseen audience of beloved and admired moral tutors and exemplars, whom

we do not wish to disappoint or morally betray, by betraying the standards of worth they have imparted to us.

A positive sense of shame flowers in a multitude of virtues, with humility the most basic. By alerting us to the limits of our strength and gifts, shame keeps us humble. Humility is a realistic and flexible sense of self which bends before adversity and even failure, but does not shatter. A healthy sense of shame allows us to be humbled, without being humiliated. Both of these words share the same root: *humus*, or earth. We *humans* (same root) belong to the earth; contact with humility need not stain or shame us.

In our efforts of love and work we can expect to stumble. We are brought down to earth from our lofty ideals as we meet the limits of our courage and generosity. We bend under our commitments and are brought low in exhaustion. All this is humbling, but not necessarily humiliating. We can taste defeat without losing our worth. Humbled by our limits and brought back to earth, we learn the crucial lessons that come as humility's gift.

A healthy sense of shame matures in the virtue of dignity. In dignity we recognize the value of our embodied selves. This virtue develops slowly as we come to a greater comfort with who we are—our gifts and limits, our strengths and enduring doubts. Dignity is the esteem in which we hold ourselves. And dignity is self-respect: how we see ourselves, our comfort with the particular person we are turning out to be.

If shame as a destructive emotion is a debilitating sense of inadequacy, dignity is an enduring awareness of our worth. As this inner resource develops, we are less susceptible to others' ability to belittle or shame us. This virtue guides us through troubling, even traumatic times.

Dignity is that sense of personal integrity against which the ploys of social shaming cannot prevail. Russian dissident Natan Sharansky has described the insight into humiliation forced upon him by the intrusive interrogations of the KGB:

> On that occasion, when I was stripped and searched, I decided it was best to treat my captors like the weather. A storm can cause you troubles, and sometimes those problems can be humiliating. But the storm itself doesn't humiliate you. Once I understood this

I realized that nothing they did could humiliate me. I could only humiliate myself—by doing something I might later be ashamed of . . . *Nothing they can do can humiliate me. I alone can humiliate myself.*

In the trauma of his crisis, Sharansky refuses to be shamed. Plutarch's proverb is proved true even in such straits: "We can remove our clothes without removing our sense of shame." A sense of dignity becomes so ingrained that it cannot be stripped away.

Twenty-five years ago a gathering of gay and lesbian Catholics chose *Dignity* as the name of their new organization. Dignity members were keenly aware how society's harassment stripped them of self-respect and instilled a profound sense of worthlessness. Shamed by civic and religious authorities, homosexual and bisexual men and women traditionally retreated into closets of silence and self-hatred. Such self-hatred often provoked behavior that seemed to justify society's condemnation. Now with local chapters throughout the country and a national office for resources and coordination, Dignity/USA has lived up to its name, supporting lesbians and gay men in their liberation from the prison of shame into the world of self-respect, mutual support, public service and advocacy.

Chastity

Shame guards the boundaries of our sexual bodies. Dignity takes root in our body as the virtue of chastity. Chastity is the well-honed sensitivity that balances intimacy and solitude in our life, that guides our decisions about sexual expression.

This virtue is not the same as abstinence or celibacy. Chastity is an inner sense of modesty that protects us as we attempt to both reveal and conceal ourselves. In the words of Carl Schneider, "the sense of shame is that space-creating hesitation that allows us to know one another without brusqueness or intrusion." Our matured sense of shame keeps the volatile energy of sexuality fully human: that is, respectful and mutual. Deprived of this seasoned instinct of shame, sexual excitement can erupt into abusive and obscene actions.

Chastity is the matured sense of shame that guides our exposure to one another. When we show ourselves to another person we want this to be an act of revelation: we extend our heart as well as our body.

Chastity is that healthy hesitance that helps love catch up with passion, so that they might go hand in hand in sexual sharing.

Humility, dignity, and chastity: virtues that shape the movements of our hearts and bodies. Guided by these resources we gradually become more graceful in our movements toward and away from others. A sense of shame becomes a grace—a skillful confidence in the dance of human interaction.

But we think of shame more often in its negative guise—feeling ashamed or disgraced. When the grace of a positive sense of shame has been stolen from us, we are left unsure of how to act, of what we are worth. We move clumsily and awkwardly when we approach others. Susceptible to others' intrusions, we are easy prey to those who would take advantage of us. We live not in grace but on the edge of disgrace. Yet even here, will and warrior arouse us to reclaim the gift of a healthy sense of shame that safeguards our dignity.

Reflective Exercise

Consider some of the ordinary expressions of adult will power: forcefulness, determination, self-control, persistence, self-confidence, stubbornness, resolve. Then recall a recent experience of your own exercise of personal will; take time to bring the memory fully to mind.

Now reflect on these questions: How did this exercise of will power enhance or strengthen you? Did this exercise of personal will challenge or distress you in any way? Did *shame* or *embarrassment* play any part in this experience—inhibiting you, threatening you, goading you to act, making you more sensitive to the context or consequences of your actions?

Finally, spend a few moments taking notes on your own sense of the connections between shame and will.

Additional Resources

We are especially grateful to Carl Schneider for his insightful exploration of the positive resource of shame in *Shame, Exposure and Privacy*; in our chapter we quote from p. 16. Bernard Williams recovers the role of a healthy virtue of shame in *Shame and Necessity*. Williams is intent to rescue the early Greek sensitivity to shame from its negative evaluation by many historians as "pre-moral" social conformity; see especially his discussion of "Shame and Autonomy" in chapter 4.

Erik Erikson discusses the development of will in *Identity and the Life Cycle*, pp. 70–71. Michael Lewis advances the developmental approach in his positive treatment of shame in *Shame: The Exposed Self*. Robert Moore and Douglas Gillette explore the Jungian archetype of the warrior in *King, Warrior, Magician, Lover*. For Natan Sharansky's observation about humiliation, see his autobiography *Fear No Evil*, p. 8. Sidney Callahan's observation linking healthy shame and mature conscience appears in her *In Good Conscience*, p. 64.

Novelist Milan Kundera's description of shyness appears in his short story "The Hitchhiking Game." For Adam Phillips's reflections on composure, see *On Kissing, Tickling, and Being Bored: Psychoanalytic Essays on the Unexamined Life*, pp. 42 and following. Stephanie Dowrick documents the sensitivities to exposure and distance required for genuine intimacy in *Intimacy and Solitude: Balancing Closeness and Independence*.

In his discussion of spirituality, *Taking a Chance on God*, John McNeill looks at shame's relevance to the religious experience of lesbian and gay Christians. Lewis B. Smedes explores shame's healthy dimensions in *Shame and Grace: Healing the Shame We Don't Deserve*; see especially chapters 4 and 8.

9

The Guises of Guilt

Guilt is the guardian of our goodness.
Willard Gaylin

A rumor circulates these days that guilt is bad. How the rumor got started is easy to understand. For all of us, feeling guilty is unpleasant. And sometimes feeling guilty seems downright irrational: we are filled with remorse about an action that we know is not wrong or racked with guilt over situations for which we are not personally responsible. This ruinous mood recruits us to the chorus condemning guilt.

But there is more to it. Feeling guilty is a uniquely human response; without this "necessary disturbance" the species would be at risk. As psychiatrist Willard Gaylin says, "we are so constructed that we must serve the social good—on which we are dependent for survival—and when we do not, we suffer the pangs of guilt."

Guilt, then, is the price of belonging. In love and work we willingly forge bonds that give our life purpose and pleasure. And, being human, we sometimes fail these bonds. When we neglect the promises we have made or turn away from people to whom we are pledged, the emotion of guilt signals that something has gone awry.

Genuine guilt is a companion of commitment. But this positive resource sometimes distorts into a destructive mood. A hardworking executive, successful at her job, struggles with an abiding sense that she is somehow blameworthy. She is filled with regret—but for what? This faceless misgiving seeps into her soul, sapping enthusiasm and joy from her life.

A young man feels vaguely guilty about his sexuality. No particular transgression troubles him; rather he is suspicious of any sensual delight and hesitant about the attractions he feels. His guilt is less about *doing* something than about *being* a sexual person.

In these examples the healthy emotion of guilt sickens into a mood of self-punishment. Psychologists and self-help authors rightfully condemn this kind of guilt and urge us to free our lives of its force. But guilt comes in many guises. Befriending this emotion demands distinguishing genuine guilt from the distortions that bear the same name.

Genuine Guilt

I left the house feeling terrible. I tried to put the argument out of my mind, but the feelings would not go away. Finally I had to admit it; I had hurt Angie very much. How could I have so ignored and then insulted her—the person I love most in the world! But I had. An hour later I went back into the house, found Angie and asked her forgiveness. We talked about my tendency to take her for granted, about her sarcasm, about how busy both our schedules have become. We talked about how we could start to change some of ways we hurt each other. I left for work later with a whole range of feelings: gratitude that we were together again, sorrow for my repeated failure, mellowness about how difficult it is to love well.

When we injure a loved one, when we undermine our best values, we feel guilty. Genuine guilt is an arousal of the heart, an alarm that warns us of a wound we have inflicted. This healthy emotion has four characteristics. First, the alarm begins in the awareness that we have failed in a particular way. Genuine guilt focuses on concrete behavior, the actions and omissions by which we have hurt other people or ourselves. Second, we recognize that a significant relationship has been damaged—a relationship with someone else or with our own deepest values. Third, we admit that we are responsible; our behavior is at fault. Finally, this acknowledgement impels us to action. Authentic guilt leads us to reestablish contact with those we have hurt and to renew the bonds between us. If shame makes us want to hide from other people, "guilt," psychiatrist Willard Gaylin suggests, "wants exposure."

Genuine guilt also motivates us to make amends. Its pain prompts us to apologize for injuries we have caused and to correct our behavior in the future. Without guilt's insistence, we would be less likely to hold ourselves accountable to the commitments that shape our life.

Inauthentic Guilt

After ten years teaching history in a multi-cultural high school, Gregory applied for a professional leave and secured funding covering a full year's salary. Looking forward to the time on his own, Greg had planned a full range of activities—time for reading and possibly some writing, visits to libraries with important collections in his field, travel for fun with his wife and their two children. But about a month into the new schedule, Gregory felt increasingly uneasy and unproductive. "It took me a couple of weeks to identify the mood: I was feeling guilty. I felt like I was letting someone down—but who?" The mood continued, taking up more of Greg's attention and exhausting him. "I had this growing sense of how selfish I was. Here I am on leave, while my friends and colleagues at school have to face the daily drudgery of their jobs. My wife, an emergency room nurse, doesn't get time away. If I were more generous, I wouldn't need this time off; if I were more creative, I'd already be making real progress on my sabbatical project. Some days I almost enjoyed being absorbed in this sense of guilt. The mood enveloped me. Sometimes I'd snap at Julie or the kids for keeping me from my projects but most of the time I just felt depressed. There seemed to be no escape."

Guilt feelings signal that we have done something wrong. Genuine guilt focuses on the offending behavior and motivates us to change. Inauthentic guilt distracts us from the concrete details of what we have done by absorbing us in how bad we are. When the focus shifts from "I have failed here" to "I *am* a failure," guilt goes awry.

Author Joan Borysenko makes the distinction between these two tendencies:

> Healthy guilt opens the way to increasing our self-awareness, resolving our difficulties, improving our relationships, and growing spiritually, [while] unhealthy guilt keeps us stuck in a continual restatement of our presumed unworthiness.

False guilt distracts us from what we can do to make things better. When its arousal turns increasingly inward, guilt becomes a curse.

Genuine guilt is a social emotion, warning us of relationships we have injured and impelling us to make amends. To concentrate on ourselves as culprits obscures these social goals. This self-condemnation feeds a sense that we are helpless in guilt's grasp. Feeling unworthy derails us, diverting energy instead into punishing ourselves. Preoccupied by our personal distress, we lose sight of the social dimensions of our pain.

When Guilt Goes Wrong

My guilt pursues me like a small snapping dog. When guilt lunges at me, I back away. Then I throw out morsels—little achievements, duties done, good works accomplished—to placate the guilt and distract it from attacking me. But guilt just consumes my peace offerings and keeps on going! There must be a better way to deal with this little monster!

Guilt's destructiveness lies in its ability to tyrannize our life. Only slowly do we notice that corrosive guiltiness has seized control. A chief characteristic of destructive guilt is compulsiveness. To overcome a sense of guiltiness, we fill our days with tasks, duties, and good works. We become compulsive helpers, driven to respond to every need that presents itself. And we find it almost impossible to say "no." What criteria could we use to refuse others' requests? No external criteria seem to work since the needs in the world are endless. What internal criteria can we rely on? Colds, flu, headaches, and exhaustion become the sole indicators of the limits of our responsibility.

When guilt goes wrong, we are bedeviled by the terror of letting other people down. We don't want to offend, to hurt feelings, to disappoint. So we comply with all requests, letting everybody write their names on our dance card. This destructive behavior enslaves us to conformity. Our eagerness to avoid offense is rooted less in personal principle than in a need to meet others' expectations.

Compulsiveness becomes evident in our speech. We salt our conversation with "should" and "have to," rarely examining the source of these "shoulds." And regretting our inadequacy, we constantly apologize. Even our generosity comes wrapped in apologies: giving a dear friend a birthday gift, we make sure to include the receipt, convinced in advance that she will want to exchange whatever we have chosen for something nicer.

Compulsiveness often takes the form of perfectionism, an affliction sometimes confused with virtue. Calling someone a perfectionist may be meant as a compliment, meaning she has high ideals, won't accept slipshod work, demands the best in life. And the addiction of perfectionism receives considerable support in an achievement-oriented society. Americans, for example, tend to admire the workaholic executive who keeps long hours and accomplishes many tasks.

In fact, perfectionism is a compulsion driven by guilt, sapping our life of pleasure and enjoyment. This fretting preoccupation to get everything right refuses to accept our limited humanity. A friend, very successful in his career but also harassed by perfectionism, tells this story on himself. After giving a lecture to forty professional colleagues, he checked their written evaluations to discover that thirty eight participants had deeply appreciated the talk and two persons had found it only mildly useful. The rest of the day he worried about these two "lost sheep." What did they not like? Perhaps he could track them down, explain his lecture again, and they would be satisfied. The price of his punitive worry is that he takes little pleasure in his work. Guilt drives out delight. Obsessed with every limitation and upset with any shortcoming, perfectionists seldom permit themselves to feel proud, to rejoice, or to be grateful.

Compulsive guilt is a chain letter that must keep going! Every addiction—for attention or food or sex—has an endless hunger. We feed it more and more, but we always come up short since we are trying to satisfy an insatiable appetite. Destructive guilt's only remedy is to give up the driven quest for "getting it right" or "doing enough." Saint Augustine, who knew something about compulsions and guilt, describes the moment of his conversion: "I let up on myself a little." For many of us this is where healing begins.

Reaching for High Ideals

The seeds of unhealthy guilt may lie in the peculiar dynamics of our best ideals. Early in our childhood, parents and teachers exhort us to be generous, to study hard, to do our work carefully. Society sets out lofty models for us to emulate: judges, nurses, astronauts, scholars, saints. In our teens and twenties we internalize these cultural ideals to support our own adult vocation.

These early ideals of achievement and service stretch us, expanding both ambition and generosity. But in our thirties and forties we face a different challenge. Now the task is to make these universal values fit our particular life; we need to personalize our ideals. During these decades, life instructs us in that mix of talent and limitation, of bravery and fear we have turned out to be. We wince, recognizing the unavoidable gap between our early ideals and how our life actually unfolds. Only *this* large-hearted, only *this* capable, only *this* wise—more perhaps than we had once believed, but limited nonetheless.

When all is going well, this sober realization doesn't cause grave disappointment. We acknowledge our ideals have done their work, enlarging and enriching us. Maturing, we recognize our early goals were necessarily larger than life. Our not being the perfect parent or the business success or the sports hero we imagined, is now neither a terrible failure nor a source of guilt. Grateful for their contribution, we need not turn ideals into cudgels for punishing ourself. But, of course, sometimes we do. When we fail to personalize our ideals, these values never *become* us. They remain in us as foreign bodies, aggravating guilt rather than nourishing us.

Keeping Guilt in Bounds

Authentic guilt operates within the boundaries of responsibility and forgiveness. Like powerful hands, these seasoned impulses hold guilt in check.

Responsibility

Our guilt extends only as far as we feel responsible; without this sense of responsibility there is no guilt. Consider an extreme example—the sociopath who lacks the capacity for empathy and mistreats other people without remorse. A person like this, without effective emotional links to other people, is dangerously disconnected from society. The attachments and duties that bind us to one another forge a sense of shared humanity. Shorn of this sensitivity, a person feels no responsibility for his social actions and hence, no guilt.

But most of us suffer a quite different affliction: we are more likely to feel *too* responsible. Trained to be dependable and encouraged to respond to other people's needs, we are alert to the troubles, shortcomings and failures that plague human living. Christine gives an example:

> A colleague came by my desk in the office yesterday and asked if I had a pair of scissors he could borrow. "No," I said. Then I added, "I'm sorry." And that's really how I felt—guilty, like I had somehow let him down.

Tony's example is different but his feelings are similar.

> Last weekend when I was cleaning my desk at home I came across a stack of requests from worthy causes. I really feel bad when these appeals for money come in the mail. Financially, I'm not able to respond to more than a few. But I feel guilty about not sending money to the other groups. So instead of tossing away the other requests as they come in, I let them pile up on my desk! I know it's crazy, but throwing them all away once a year is easier for me.

How do we learn the limits of our responsibility? When we are children, parents introduce us to the range of our accountability, reminding us to keep our word and to care for our siblings. As we mature our responsibility expands: we undertake new commitments and pursue larger ideals. But as the boundary of our responsibility expands, it also contracts: we learn about the limits of our strengths and gifts. We cannot do everything or remedy all the woes of the world. Even as we take on new cares we must let go dreams that no longer fit our life. Thus do we learn about the edges of our responsibility: the grey area where our duties end and the somber place where our ideals meet the limits of our resources and calling.

But boundaries between ourselves and others, signposts of both our responsibility and our guilt, remain permeable. In empathy we cross the line that separates us from others, now feeling their pain or sharing their joy. Empathy with another's sorrow makes us eager to relieve the distress. When we cannot improve this person's life, we sometimes feel guilty. Our compassion mushrooms into a false sense of responsibility: we *should* be able to change another person's life! A healthy impulse of empathy heads toward unhealthy guilt.

Women are culturally susceptible to this distortion. Social norms convince many women that their particular vocation is to care for their children, support their spouses, and listen to their neighbors' troubles.

If her calling is to care for others, where can a woman draw the line? Facing this boundless responsibility overwhelms her. In such a cultural climate, care for others continually outranks care for self. So when personal illness or exhaustion compel her to pay attention to herself, she feels considerable guilt.

Maturity challenges us to forge a sense of responsibility that acknowledges its own limits: We alone are not responsible for the world. The limits of our responsibility, defined by our finite resources and commitments already pledged, need not blind us to others' pain. But our calling is to solidarity, not to false guilt.

Forgiveness

Forgiveness is the other boundary that holds our guilt in check. Failing a relationship or commitment, healthy guilt impels us to make amends. And this same emotion moves us to ask forgiveness. A friend writes:

> I feel miserable. Last week I let down a good friend. The next day I went to her, told her I was sorry and asked her to forgive me. We had a good long talk, setting things straight between us. When I left, Sylvia let me know I was forgiven. That evening I stopped at church on the way home and asked God's forgiveness as well. Today I still feel miserable. I am so disappointed with myself. How could I have offended Sylvia like that? I know she has forgiven me, but I can't let go of the experience. It's almost that I *want* to feel bad for awhile! Why do I hold onto this guilt?

Guilt fails us when we are unable to ask for forgiveness or remain convinced we do not merit pardon. Here, as when we feel responsible for the whole world, we make ourselves very important. In both instances we ignore a boundary designed to contain this dangerous emotion.

When guilt is embraced by an act of forgiveness, the painful feeling begins to dissolve; we are absolved of our guilt. Making restitution is part of seeking forgiveness: we give back the money or repay an emotional debt. But sometimes rebalancing is not easy. What restitution makes up for the abuse of an alcoholic parent or the injury of a violent spouse? Face-to-face reconciliation isn't possible with antagonists long dead. Some wrongs cannot be put right by repayments; then only the gift of forgiveness heals.

The gospel tells a story of such forgiveness. A crowd hungry for vengeance and public humiliation surrounds the woman accused of adultery. They goad Jesus to condemn her as the law demands but he seems strangely uninterested in their righteous fervor. Jesus questions the crowd's credentials for rendering lethal judgment: "Let the one who is without sin throw the first stone." Confused and disappointed, her accusers drift away. Jesus does not condemn her. Instead he urges her to avoid her self-destructive behavior and then supports her on her way. His gracious attitude seems to dispel both her guilt and her shame. This is the surprise and renewal of forgiveness: the spell is broken. Forgiveness heals our history and dissolves our guilt.

A Question Of Conscience

Erik Erikson describes conscience as "the great governor of initiative." In Erikson's vision of human development, children between four and seven are learning much about initiative. Now stronger in body and more capable in language and imagination, children express themselves more forcefully. But in a world with other people, taking initiative sometimes means intrusion: we collide with others, invade their preserve, overturn their tranquillity.

To survive we need to learn the limits of our initiative. We must develop the ability to recognize where we have gone too far and pushed too hard. This crucial ability to regulate self we call conscience. The reliable resource of conscience is the cornerstone of morality. Only if trustworthy values are personalized in our conscience can we trust ourselves to distinguish between right and wrong. Erikson describes the fruit of this interior strength: ". . . that dependence on [my]self which makes [me], in turn, dependable."

Conscience has traced a tortuous cultural journey. Sigmund Freud argued that guilt is a necessary neurosis, the high price we must pay for repressing the primitive impulses of sex and aggression. As sociologist Philip Rieff explains, conscience for Freud "is furnished by social authority and remains, unreflectively, at authority's disposal." In this understanding, conscience "civilizes" us by grafting society's demands onto our selfish psyches.

In an individualistic society like ours, conscience can mean quite the opposite: independent private judgment, free of all social constraints. Here conscience becomes a privileged authority separated from the external demands of social institutions. Its interior autonomy legitimizes a boundless insistence on rights of privacy and self-expression.

Jewish and Christian wisdom has always envisioned conscience as more than social constraint or individual autonomy. Personal conscience originates in the cultural and religious values that parents and teachers instill in us. But for conscience to mature, we must personalize these ideals. Reaffirming some, rejecting others, we integrate our best hopes and beliefs in our particular calling.

Every conscience is social. In this reservoir of values, the ideals of our family and faith survive and thrive. Our conscience is a repository and witness to the goodness we have inherited. But our conscience is social in a second sense. This interior strength not only serves our own life; conscience is what we hand on to our children as our best wisdom.

The Voice of Conscience

A dangerous but attractive metaphor for conscience is *voice*. This image is perilous because many of us experience unhealthy guilt as authority's threatening voice within us: "do it this way or you will be punished." Psychologically disturbed persons excuse their destructive behavior by explaining that "a voice" told them to do it. Yet our healthy conscience acts like a voice, urging us toward certain decisions and warning us when we have failed our own best ideals.

Through our teens and early twenties we struggle to find our voice: the ability to express our deepest wishes for our life, to enact our best hopes with clarity and conviction. The ideals of teachers and mentors resonate in decisions that appear to us most personal. As the unique voice of our own conscience grows more confident, it harmonizes the many voices of those who have cared for us.

If conscience speaks, it also listens. Our voice becomes authentic and mature only if we listen well—to needs in our society, hopes in the immediate community, wounds in our own hearts. When we listen well, we feel the resonance of our good choices with those of our companions; and we hear these same friends challenge us when our decisions are harmful or ill-advised. In such a listening community, the voice of conscience becomes a trustworthy resource both for us and for others.

Conscience is the gradually developed ability to hear the imperatives that arise around us, to be aware of the boundaries of our responsibility, and to voice our response. For our conscience to mature into a reliable resource we will need to befriend our negative emotions. When we are smothered in shame or burdened by unhealthy guilt, our conscience cannot be trusted to make the right choice. Through the long discipline of naming and taming our negative emotions, we form our conscience and find our voice.

Even as we develop a finely tuned conscience, we can expect to suffer the lingering tremors of residual guilt. Despite our efforts to heal our perfectionism and trust our own judgments, guilt may remain a companion on the journey. We abide in a world scarred with sin and injury. Some of us know the guilt that endures after a divorce. We see the harmful effects on our children of a necessary decision, effects that our sorrow cannot erase. Even with forgiveness, this feeling of guilt endures. Or perhaps we are responsible for an accident in which other people are injured. Our contrition does not give them back their health; regret and remorse continue. Survivors of tragedies in which others have died recount their feelings of guiltiness. Why did they survive? They have no right to go on living. Each day brings fresh guilt. Despite time and forgiveness, guilt endures.

Original Guilt

Like original sin, this negative emotion reminds us of the mysteriousness of human malice. Its roots run deeper in us than we will ever fully fathom. *Original guilt* is the sorrowful responsibility that we share with others for our common inhumanity. This feeling is evoked by newsreels of atrocities inflicted in civil wars, by unending accounts of urban violence, by remembered images of concentration camps, by the sight of the homeless and hungry in our own country. It is an experience of collective guilt rooted in the undeniable ways in which human beings continue to harm one another.

Initially, most of us are reluctant to share responsibility for the ancient and continuing injustice in human life. "I am not personally to blame," we protest, "for racism or poverty or terrorism." But maturity brings many of us to acknowledge that we belong to and are active members of this wounded and wounding species. We need less and less to deny our involvement in this shared history of sin and guilt. Such an acknowledgement needn't lead us to wallow in a mood of hopelessness. The painful recognition of original guilt can both rekindle our commitment to work for justice and bring us to a tolerance blessed by patient resolve. And this uncomfortable sentiment may turn us, as believers, to our God who does not cease to forgive even such a people. Original guilt is a bad feeling that is good for us to know.

Reflective Exercise

Return to the two biblical metaphors we discussed in Chapter 3: *breaking the covenant* and *missing the mark*. Consider ways these two images are part of your experience of guilt. To start, spend several minutes in a reflective mood, becoming aware of significant times you have felt guilty. You may wish to take some notes for yourself. Be gentle with this reflection; the goal is insight not self-punishment.

Next, consider which image—*missing the mark* or *breaking the covenant*—best captures these experiences of guilt for you. Give some examples of how this is the case. Again, taking notes may help you stay with the reflection.

Then, focus on the two metaphors themselves. As you see it, how does the image *breaking the covenant* heal or purify your own sense of guilt? Are there risks in this image, at least for you?

In your experience, how does the image *missing the mark* heal or purify guilt? For you, are there risks in understanding guilt this way?

Additional Resources

Willard Gaylin offers his positive evaluation of guilt in *Feelings: Our Vital Signs*, see pp. 40 and following. In *Guilt Is the Teacher, Love Is the Lesson*, therapist Joan Borysenko gives a clear analysis of guilt and shame and provides reflective exercises to help deal with these emotions. One drawback in Borysenko's approach is her severe dichotomy of religion and spirituality; she distinguishes a generic spirituality of healthy guilt from "religious guilt [which] is the most extreme form of unhealthy guilt" (p. 27). In *What's So Bad about Guilt?*, Harlan J. Wechsler provides a more balanced reflection on religion's role; his analyses of perfectionism and what we have called "original guilt" are especially helpful; see also Gerald May's valuable work in *Addiction and Grace*.

Erik Erikson offers a heuristic exploration of the developmental tension between guilt and initiative in *Identity and the Life Cycle*; we take his comment on conscience from p. 84. In *Bringing Up a Moral Child*, psychologists Michael Schulman and Eve Mekler help parents and other caregivers understand guilt's ambiguous role. Sidney Callahan gives an illuminating discussion of conscience and the role of emotions in the development of this resource in her valuable work, *In Good Conscience*. *The Splendor of Truth* (*Veritatis Splendor*), Pope John Paul II's recent encyclical on morality, examines the "voice of conscience" as it echoes God's own voice within our own best desires; see especially pp. 314–16. We discuss the characteristics of faith communities that help form mature conscience in *Community of Faith: Crafting Christian Communities Today*.

In *Guilt: Issues of Emotional Living in an Age of Stress*, pastoral counselor Kathleen Kelley brings together a series of helpful essays on this topic. Psychologist David Burns distinguishes remorse that "stems from the undistorted awareness" of a wrongdoing from guilt that, for him, includes the sense not only of doing wrong but *being bad*; see his *Feeling Good*, pp. 178 and following. Dealing more directly with pessimism than guilt, Martin Seligman's *Learned Optimism* nevertheless offers practical help in confronting the negative self-messages and self-doubt that are often part of false guilt. Paul Tournier's *Guilt and Grace* abounds in wisdom concerning both healthy and unhealthy guilt.

In *Freud: The Mind of the Moralist*, Philip Rieff distinguishes "the religious view of conscience as intelligent and reflective as well as passionate" from Freud's conviction that "conscience is furnished by social authority and remains, unreflectively, at authority's disposal" (p. 299). For important philosophical discussions of guilt, see Paul Ricoeur's *The Symbolism of Evil*, especially pp. 100–150, and Richard Swinburne's *Responsibility and Atonement*.

Part Four

TRANSFORMING OUR PASSIONS

The Chinese character for change (hua)
includes biological alterations, cultural changes,
and spiritual transformations

10

An Angry Spirituality

Yahweh is tender and compassionate,
Slow to anger, most loving;
God's indignation does not last forever,
God's resentment exists only a short time.

Psalm 103 (JB)

Passions abound in the capacious heart of God. In the story of the great flood, God's heart is awash in disappointment: "And the Lord regretted having made humankind on the earth, and it grieved God to the heart" (Gen. 6:6). Jesus, the Son of God, suffered the full range of human emotions. He became incensed at his friend Peter; he wept at the tomb of Lazarus; he cried out with something like despair in his final moments on the cross. The Jewish and Christian Scriptures show us a God immersed in all the passions that accompany commitment. The revelation seems to be that passions are the price of love. To be entwined in others' lives is to court sorrow as well as delight, to taste loneliness as well as communion, to come to grief as well as to gratitude.

Yet this revelation has been contested. For nearly two thousand years Christians have argued about the place of passion in our lives. Is anger a natural enemy of spirituality? Are grief and loneliness distorted emotions that jeopardize our life of faith? Or are these painful stirrings wellsprings of our vitality, alerting us to endangered values and linking us to this passionate God? Early Christian thinkers, scandalized by the force of human emotion, gradually became convinced that the fleshly

passions of anger, grief, and sexual arousal separate us from our spiritual Creator.

A Dispassionate God

"God himself, according to the Scriptures, becomes angry and yet is
never disturbed by any passions whatsoever." This surprising sentence
in Augustine's *City of God* echoes the stoic ideal of total serenity.
Intimidated by their stoic critics, Christian thinkers worried forth a
strikingly unscriptural vision of a serene God, unperturbed by emotion,
safely removed from the murky, compromising drama of human
feelings.

In this portrait we are introduced to a God who loves us, but does
not need us; an "unmoved mover" who touches creatures with affection
and forgiveness, but is himself unmoved. Today we see more clearly
that this portrait is less a theology than a masculine fantasy: the ideal
of being able to care for others while remaining untouched by them;
the aspiration to provide protection and correction without being made
vulnerable to the perils of mutuality. Having been created in God's
image, men now sought to return the favor, casting God in their
likeness.

The stoic ideal of a detached love developed into a theology of
God's impassibility—God as unable to be stirred or aroused or made
vulnerable. Such a doctrine was, of course, unbelievable and most
Christians simply ignored it in favor of a scriptural God of fierce feelings. But this theology did spawn a spirituality for Christian leaders.
Ministers and priests learned that to be like God they ought to rise
above their emotions; they should craft a life detached from the swirl
of anger and fear and sexual arousal. A holy leader, this logic suggested,
influences others with care and correction, but remains unswayed by
any passionate attachment to them. To be a good leader demands
mastery of one's feelings.

Anger—The Scriptural Account

The stoic vision of a God of control diverges sharply from the biblical
image of a God of desire. Throughout the Hebrew Scriptures we encounter a God who is stirred by both anger and compassion. These

twin passions are the compass that charts God's tumultuous interaction with humankind.

Images of God's anger abound. "Then Yahweh's anger flamed out against Israel. God handed them over to pillagers who plundered them; God delivered them to the enemies surrounding them, and they were not able to resist them" (Judg. 2:14, (JB)). The prophet Zephaniah pictures God as even more incensed: "For my decision is to gather nations, to assemble kingdoms, to pour out upon them my indignation, *all the heat of my anger*, for in the fire of my passion all the earth shall be consumed" (Zeph. 3:1–8, our emphasis).

Hebrew Scripture remembers God's passionate anger as a just response, triggered by the maddening inconstancy of the very people God has chosen. Yet this anger is constantly balanced by compassion: "My compassion grows warm and tender. I will not execute my fierce anger" (Hos. 11:8); "Yahweh is tender and compassionate, slow to anger, most loving; God's indignation does not last forever" (Ps. 103, JB). For those who espouse a dispassionate Deity, God's compassion presents as much a problem as does God's anger. In Hebrew, "compassion" and "womb" share the same root; this emotion is a gut-wrenching implication in the grief of others.

Anger enjoyed a privileged place in the community of ancient Israel. The prophets often relied on anger to fuel their indictment of the fickle Israel. Jeremiah, a truly irascible personality, announced Yahweh's ire—"My anger and my wrath shall be poured out on this place" (Jer. 7:20)—and admitted that this fuming emotion had penetrated his own heart—"I am full of the wrath of the Lord and I am weary of holding it in" (Jer. 6:11).

At this point in Judeo-Christian history, the prophets represented a potent political element within the religious community. Acting as a counterbalance to the authority of the king and the priests, the prophets raised painful questions about fidelity, stagnation, and change. Prophecy made anger legitimate within the household of Israel. Even when the prophets were dismissively ignored or violently silenced, their vocation gave witness to the honorable place of anger among our religious ancestors. Their continuing presence argued that dissent and conflict have a place among God's people.

Jesus belongs in this long line of prophets. Though piety sometimes prefers the memory of Jesus as meek and humble of heart, the gospels recall an often angry person. The most familiar story recounts Jesus finding merchants setting up shop at the entrance to the temple. Outraged, he trashes their display booths. "Then Jesus went into the Temple and drove out all those who were selling and buying in the Temple and he overturned the tables of the money changers and the seats of those who were sold doves" (Matt. 21:12).

The gospels repeatedly recall Jesus' vehemence against those he judged to be hypocrites (see Luke 6:42 and Matt. 7:5; also Matt. 6:16). When some in the crowd baited him about bending the strict laws about activity on the Sabbath in order to heal a woman, he responds angrily: "You hypocrites!" (Luke 13:14). They are willing to water their ox or donkey on the Sabbath, but self-righteously insist that a suffering person go unhealed.

The Gospel of Mark recalls another time that Jesus' critics taunted him about healing on the Sabbath (Mark 3:5). Their narrow interpretation of religious laws infuriates him: "He looked around at them *with anger*; he was grieved at their hardness of heart." All three Synoptic authors—Matthew, Mark, and Luke—tell this story, showing their reliance on a common source. But at the mention of Jesus' anger, the stories diverge. Matthew's account (12:12) does not mention Jesus' angry look. Luke (6:10) repeats the phrase "He looked around at them," but without the adverb "angrily." Do we see here the first editorial attempt to disassociate Jesus from this questionable emotion?

If Jesus was angered by hypocrites and the self-righteous, he was—like us—also sparked to anger by his loved ones. Matthew's gospel recounts a poignant memory of this "intimate anger." Shortly before his death Jesus prepared to go to Jerusalem, a decision he sensed was fraught with danger. Apprehensive—but convinced he must make the trip—Jesus shares his plan with his closest companions. His friend Peter, keenly aware of the hostile atmosphere in Jerusalem, warns him not to go. Jesus suddenly explodes in anger: "Get behind me, Satan! You are a stumbling block to me" (Matt. 16:23). Harsh language for a dear friend, denouncing him as the devil. Jesus' anger reveals how vulnerable he felt in this difficult moment of decision. Fearful but determined, he looked to his friends for support only to find Peter offering him exactly the wrong advice. Jesus' anger flared to help him resist this tempting alternative and to keep his painful decision on course.

The testimony of God's wrath, the witness of the prophets' rage, the images of an angry Jesus—these arousals show us anger as more than moral failure. But what about our own anger? For Jews and Christians, the biblical evidence seems to insist, anger cannot be rejected out-of-hand. The goal instead, as captured by the psalmist and echoed in Paul's advice to the believers in Ephesus, is to "be angry and do not sin" (Ps. 4:4; Eph. 4:26).

A Deadly Sin

In the second and third centuries, the conversation about anger took a new turn. Stoicism's powerful influence in the Mediterranean world penetrated Christian belief and practice. Philosophers argued that the ideal of human life was serenity and emotional control. Human passions, whether sexual arousal, envy, or grief, were seen as major obstacles to the achievement of self-restraint and calm. Marcus Aurelius, for example, saw anger as essentially an irritable by-product of social life, a negative emotion we can well do without. Book Two of his *Meditations* begins with a musing that will sound familiar to the citizens of any large city today:

> Say to yourself in the morning: I shall meet people who are interfering, ungracious, insolent, full of guile, deceitful and antisocial: they have all become like that because they have no understanding of good and evil.

The passion most often inflamed in the course of such a day, whether in the second century or our own, is anger. Marcus Aurelius's remedy was the stoic conviction that we are all part of Nature's design, living and dying according to its script. Getting disturbed when others play their necessary role in this common, fated drama is more than foolish; it's a waste of time.

The solution, then, is to suppress the useless emotion of social anger. "Why be angry with a man because of his body odors or bad breath?" If someone jostles us at the gym (his example!), "we do not make a case of it, or strike back or suspect him in the future of intriguing against us." Even in instances of what we have called intimate anger, Marcus Aurelius counsels dispassion: "Though I was often upset at Rusticus, I did nothing excessive which I should have repented." Elsewhere he cautions against the company that anger keeps: "never be downcast, or sneering, or angry, or suspicious." For stoics like Marcus

Aurelius, anger is simply a social irritant. To foster this feeling is a vice. In a life aimed at serenity, the disruptive passion of anger is to be turned aside. For "anger is a sign of weakness, just as much as grief."

Influenced by the stoics, Christian thinkers soon identified anger as an unhealthy disturbance that was also sinful. Influential theologians— Clement and Origen, Jerome and Augustine—heard in St. Paul's opposition of the flesh and the spirit (". . . the flesh with its passions and desires," Gal. 5:25) a condemnation of all those bodily impulses that distract us from the pursuit of God. Not surprisingly, when the first inventory of the "seven deadly sins" appeared in fifth century monasteries, anger made the list. This tradition of early Christianity continues today. In his contemporary reflection on the seven deadly sins, Henry Fairlie argues that "anger may not always cause a deep wound, but *it must leave* a residue of hatred in the end, and a desire for revenge (our emphasis)." If anger runs necessarily to rage, if vindication and revenge are indistinguishable, then surely anger is a lethal emotion.

Developments in church life contributed to the loss of a positive role for anger. In the course of the third century, for reasons that are still unclear to historians and theologians, the ancient tradition of prophecy suddenly withered and all but disappeared. For two hundred years after the death and raising of Jesus, a recognized ministry of prophecy flourished in the community of faith. Individuals arose who carried on the dangerous but necessary mission of challenging Christians to purify their lives and remain faithful to God. But by the end of the third century this charism had atrophied in the community. Many Christians believed that the age of revelation had come to an end. God had now revealed all we must know for our salvation; henceforth we need only be faithful to an already available truth. In such a climate we would not need prophets.

The essential gift of prophecy survived in Christian life, but it had to find new abodes. Some bishops led with prophetic vigor, though their primary calling as administrators and preservers of the religious institution often put them in conflict with the radical demands of prophecy. Prophecy survived in religious orders as these flowered, first in desert monasteries and eventually throughout Europe and beyond. But the institution of prophecy—the official acknowledgement of an adversarial voice within the community of faith—had perished. Its demise undermined the legitimacy of dissent and cast doubt on anger's role. Now a good case could be made that religious orthodoxy required obedient conformity to the demands of those in authority. No longer did the church expect the outrage of ancient prophets or the angry challenge of Jesus to find an echo within its own life. Henceforth, opposition would be judged a moral failing and a sign of disobedience. The loss of the charism of prophecy effectively outlawed anger.

Reclaiming a Positive Vision of Anger

For a thousand years anger's sinfulness remained a dominant Christian conviction. Then, in the thirteenth century, the conversation about this emotion took a radical turn as Thomas Aquinas developed his vision of human nature. Newly available to the scholars of this period were the ancient texts of Aristotle, in which anger appears not as an irrational impulse, but an ordinary, indispensable emotion: "We praise a person who feels anger on the right grounds and against the right persons and also in the right manner. . . ." For Aristotle, anger is a healthy, if volatile arousal that fuels a person's protest of a wrong or her resistance to injustice. The good health of both individuals and societies hinges on the ability to become angry and express this emotion in a tempered fashion.

Relying on the authority of Aristotle, Aquinas crafted a vision of human emotions that diverged from the Christian view that had prevailed for a millennium. For Aquinas, passions were not the distorted, compulsive emotions of Clement of Alexandria and Augustine, necessarily at war with reason and the spirit. Passions were healthy arousals, honorable parts of a human nature designed by the Creator. These powerful forces, when tamed, provide the vital energy that fuels human virtue. "Justice cannot be without passion, and much less other virtues."

In three chapters of his *Summa Theologiae* Aquinas used Aristotle's authority to reshape Christian attitudes toward anger. First, he shrewdly adjusted Augustine's conviction that "anger craves revenge." A healthy anger, Aquinas corrects, seeks a just vindication, rather than indiscriminate revenge. Vindication and vengeance are not to be confused. Aquinas then reinterprets Augustine's judgment that "anger grows into hatred." The impulse of anger does not swell into hatred automatically or unavoidably, but only "over time"—if and as we allow it. We can choose to block this destructive escalation. Anger and hatred are not linked lethally: hatred thirsts for evil but a healthy anger desires vindication "for the sake of justice."

Aquinas carefully traces the bonds between anger and reason. If Christians had traditionally seen this emotion as a blind impulse embedded in "the flesh," Aquinas insists that anger remains open to reason's influence. Again, he depends on Aristotle's authority: "Anger listens to reason to some extent . . . but it is not perfectly attentive." Anger is compatible with reason, because it is natural and reasonable for a person to be stirred up to resist threats of injury: "it is natural . . . to be aroused against what is hostile and threatening." Anger fails only when it ignores reason's counsel in a rush to vengeance.

In his second chapter (Question 47), Aquinas anticipates contemporary research that uncovers the connections between anger and shame: "All the motives of anger are reducible to slight." When we are belittled or forgotten, or when our dignity is slighted, we are aroused to anger. Aquinas's reflections on the link between neglect and anger have a modern feel: "neglect [*oblivio*] is an evident sign of slight; we take the trouble to remember things which are important to us." Likewise, when a special vulnerability or personal weakness is exposed, anger flares as a healthy defensive response. In his few paragraphs, Aquinas unravels what had seemed a contemporary insight: when shame diminishes us and our dignity shrinks, the arousal of anger enlarges us, to protest our loss and prevent our being forgotten.

A Revolutionary Emotion

In the third chapter (Question 48), Aquinas explores the effects of anger's physiological arousal. When we are offended, anger stirs as a "counter-irritant" to both announce and resist the injury. But this interior agitation has revolutionary potential: It may overturn our world and compel us to new behavior.

Anger is revolutionary in its ability to *expose* us. Again, Aquinas depends on Aristotle: "An angry person is not devious, but quite open." If we are aroused by anger, we may suddenly blurt out a conviction. Dropping our usual reserve, we show our emotional hand. Suddenly, everyone in the office or at the meeting knows how we feel. The spontaneous and precipitous openness that anger provokes may be harmful and a source of humiliation. But it may also be a fruitful revelation, to ourselves and others, of our own best beliefs. Aquinas interprets such impulsive self-revelation as a kind of ironic "magnanimity": "It is also partly an effect of the expansion of the heart, a function of magnanimity which is also produced by anger." The magnanimous person speaks freely and openly shows his feelings, unlike a more secretive, defensive individual. Anger, with its spontaneous "expansion of the heart," may compel us to be more magnanimous than we had planned.

When this arousal stirs us to resist an indignity and suddenly reveals our agitation to others it sets us on a course of change. If we are not prepared to face the change that anger instigates, we do well to suppress this emotion. Contemporary analysts of anger have noted this revolutionary element in anger. In her study of depression, Dana Crowley Jack underscores the lack of passion in depressed women and the radical implications of a rebirth of anger. This dangerous emotion "brings a clarity of vision and a requirement to act." The arousal of anger separates a person from the protective cocoon of depression, igniting in her the hope of a different way of living. Such changes are revolutionary because they require us to become assertive participants in our future. In *Composing a Life*, Mary Catherine Bateson notes anger's gift to her: "Anger was an achievement, a step away from the chasm of despair."

In the Company of Conflict

Anger is also revolutionary in the company it keeps. If anger is sometimes legitimate, so is conflict. Many Christians aspire to peace and harmony; we long for a calm life and an orderly society. But we do well to remember the essential role of conflict and even anger in our religious heritage. The saving journey of Jews and Christians is marked by long experiences in a hostile desert and a bruising exile, by a painful way of the cross. If harmony and calm are worthy goals, the path to these ideals is most often marked by struggle and conflict.

Our ancestors in ancient Greece used the word *agon* to signify the "agony" or "contest" of life. Whether in physical contests or political debates or philosophical disputes, the Greeks saw struggle not as a scandal but as an essential means of finding our way. In the words of philosopher Alasdair MacIntyre, these ancestors recognized that "it was in the context of the *agon* that . . . truth had to be discovered." For these Greeks, the genuine goods of life wait to be wrestled from the forces that repeatedly defeat them.

In an agonistic world of obstacles and antagonists, conflict is an unavoidable dynamic. Alasdair MacIntyre reminds us of the centrality of conflict in every heritage: "Traditions, when vital, embody continuities of conflict." Differing visions collide in a richly pluralist society, but these differences need not be fatal. Our variety energizes us to reexamine our values; our disagreements compel us to clarify our shared goals. As philosopher John Anderson has observed, "It is through conflict and sometimes only through conflict that we learn what our ends and purposes are."

Courage and Temperance

Anger often erupts as a raw, unruly emotion. To serve its best purposes, our passion requires refinement. Honing anger's arousal to the work of virtuous action is an angry spirituality's most practical task. This discipline shapes our passion into the virtues of courage and temperance.

Anger enjoys its finest moment when it fuels the courageous pursuit of justice. Courage, of course, is not always angry. One person quietly and courageously faces terminal illness; another confronts a difficult job with a steady resolve. But sometimes courage rides anger's energy. The Spanish language hints at this link in the word *coraje*—"righteous anger." Though the word names an emotion, it harbors the word courage. Just anger, it literally suggests, is a form of courage.

In his analysis of courage, Alasdair MacIntyre notes its connections with care. When persons we care for or values we cherish are threatened, we rise to their defense. Courage, MacIntyre suggests, is this "capacity to risk harm or danger to oneself" in the expression of our care. The most universal example is the parent who spontaneously— and courageously—fights any adversary to protect a child. Anger fuels this dangerous mission of care.

For theologian Josef Pieper, the links between courage and anger lie in their overlapping intents: anger is "a force directed toward the difficulty of achievement" and courage is our resolve in "facing the dreadful." Both dynamics embolden us to face painful challenges. Courage, Pieper reminds us, is not the lack of fear but the resolve to act in spite of fear. Conscious of her vulnerability, the courageous person still goes forward—for the sake of what she prizes. As Pieper suggests, courage is the willingness to proceed in the face of threat; finally, "the willingness to fall, to die in battle."

Eastern wisdom, too, reinforces the bond between anger and courage. "There are some things that I loathe more than death; that is why there are troubles I do not avoid." These words of the Chinese sage Mencius anchor his vision of courage. To explore this ancient vision, historian Lee Yearley returns us to the mysterious energy of *ch'i*. As we saw in chapter 4, this vital life force sometimes takes the shape of anger. For Mencius, the energy of *ch'i* when joined to righteousness becomes the fuel of courageous action. In Mencius's view, when we see an injustice we do not simply evaluate its evil with a cool detachment; we get angry. This passionate arousal, in league with reason, rallies us to risk ourselves in confronting the injustice. Anger's passion, Yearley notes, "can generate the added impetus that allows a person to overcome fear or some other difficulty." Mencius's linking of *ch'i* and righteousness parallels the union of anger and reason in Aquinas. When nourished and nurtured, the vital energy of *ch'i* supplies a person with an "assurance about one's goals, added energy to reach them" and helps "ensure that the tumultuous forces released by legitimate fears will be overcome."

But even in the service of courage, anger's force can go astray. Courage benefits from anger's power only if it is tempered. For many Americans today, "temperance" suggests mildness, reticence, and an absence of passion. Christian piety shares some of the blame, insinuating that the truly virtuous should absent themselves from passionate behavior. Such a conviction drains temperance of all vitality. And this hesitance about passion has a long history. In *Body and Society*, Peter Brown ✓ illustrates that very early in Christian thought "chastity" came to signify abstinence from sexual sharing, rather than a lovemaking that blends tenderness and passion.

So it was with anger. Christian temperance turned into a disciplined avoidance rather than a virtuous expression of this emotion. In a collective amnesia, Christians forgot the angry prophets. Temperance seemed to demand "turning the other cheek" and following a Jesus who was seen only as "meek and humble of heart."

But in its truest guise, temperance serves as the companion of courage. The one virtue emboldens us to act, while the other moderates our self-expression. When we are angry, we must become sufficiently aroused to resist threat and injustice without becoming violent. The metaphor of heat helps us appreciate temperance's contribution here. Anger heats us up; we get "steamed" and threaten to boil over in hostile actions. We are in danger of losing our temper. Temperance helps cool the temperature, bringing our anger down to a productive range. Avoiding the heat of anger is not temperance's only choice. We can act temperately *in the midst of* anger—moderating our rage and focusing its energy effectively. In metallurgy, "to temper" means to refine metal until it is both strong and flexible. A well-tempered piece of steel suits both a battle sword and a construction site. Our well-tempered anger, too, both protects and builds up.

Courage and temperance are not simply personal resources that we conjure out of heroic, individual effort; they are social strengths cultivated in encouraging environments. Ideally we learn to be courageous and to temper our anger by watching our family and friends and neighbors. If we come from injured and injuring homes, we may learn about boldness from sources where anger and rage are not distinguished and vindication looks very much like vengeance.

The Power of Wrath

"At the mention of anger, Christian awareness sees as a rule only the uncontrolled, the anti-spiritual, the negative aspect. But, as with 'sensuality' and 'desire,' the power of wrath also belongs to the primal forces of human nature." A generation ago, Josef Pieper sounded the call for a recovery of the healthy resource of anger. "Wrath is the strength to attack the repugnant; the power of anger is actually the power of resistance in the soul."

A Christian spirituality of anger demands public acknowledgement of its revolutionary elements. By recovering our tradition of prophecy and the memory of an irritable Jesus, we may allow this emotion to take its place among us once more. This acknowledgement will compel us to recognize that conflict plays an unavoidable role in our shared life. We can argue about our differing visions of the Christian calling without insulting or injuring one another. We can even become angry with one another and yet prevent this emotion from escalating into hatred. We can relearn the rules of civility and treat our adversaries with honor and respect.

Democratic societies have taught the world about the healthy role of the loyal opposition. We debate and oppose one another, but then go forward as colleagues, not enemies. Embedded in the notion of a loyal opposition is the virtue of civility: the strength of combining antagonism with respect, of disagreeing without degrading our opponent. Critics, from Catholic archbishop Rembert Weakland to author Scott Peck, have noted the withering of civility in America. When antagonists employ bitter invective and accuse one another of the worst motives, they erode the line between anger and hatred, between vindication and vengeance. Then the ordinary conflicts and unavoidable *agon* of social life become deadly.

A robust spirituality of anger faces a daunting future: overcoming our amnesia of irascible prophets and an angry Jesus; admitting conflict as a necessary dynamic in our religious life; disbelieving that violence can remedy our differences; recrafting civility as a political virtue; reinvigorating the ancient virtues of courage and temperance. Short of such a renaissance, we will be left with a moribund religious tradition of anger as a deadly sin and a cultural heritage of violence as the ordinary and acceptable voice of anger.

Reflective Exercise

Consider experiences of anger—yours or someone else's—in the public arena: in civic life, in politics, at work or school, within the church. First, list several instances when anger in these social settings was, in your judgment, detrimental or damaging. Concretely, what were the negative effects of these angry incidents? As you see it, what factors contributed most to making anger negative in these cases—factors in the combatants? factors in the bystanders? factors in the larger setting?

Then list examples when anger in these social settings had positive outcomes. Practically, what were the good effects you noted? What factors—people, values, attitudes, behaviors, circumstances—help anger produce these positive results here?

Now, list some of your own convictions about anger's place in public life. Finally, include your convictions about anger's place on the spiritual journey.

Additional Resources

Loughlan Sofield, Carroll Juliano, and Rosine Hammett explore anger's contribution to spirituality in *Design for Wholeness*. Dana Crowley Jack discusses the importance of personal anger in *Silencing the Self*, page

140. Mary Catherine Bateson describes anger's gift to her in *Composing a Life*, pp. 205–206. Social psychologist Deborah Tannen speaks to the disciplines of public civility in her essay "The Triumph of the Yell," which appeared in the *New York Times*, January 14, 1994; see also Scott Peck's discussion of civility in *A World Waiting to Be Born*.

Biblical scholar John McKenzie acknowledges anger as a central passion in the Hebrew Scriptures: The prophet Nathan was willing to provoke King David's anger with a story of injustice (2 Sam. 12:1–14); Ezekiel announces God's wrath (Ezek. 8:18), as does the prophet Hosea (Hos. 5:10); see *The Jerome Biblical Commentary*, p. 753. Abraham Heschel, in *The Prophets*, observes that Jeremiah could confuse his own indignation with God's anger. As a Jewish commentator, Heschel is much more comfortable with God's mood swings ("the dramatic tension in the inner life of God," p. 103) than are most Christian theologians. Theologian Phyllis Trible explains the literal link between compassion and womb in *God and the Rhetoric of Sexuality*, p. 33: "In its singular form the noun *rehem* means 'womb' or 'uterus.' In the plural, *rahmim*, this concrete meaning expands to the abstractions of compassion, mercy and love. . . . Accordingly, our metaphor lies in the semantic movement from a physical organ of the female body to a psychic mode of being."

In *Ministry: Leadership in the Community of Jesus Christ* Edward Schillebeeckx chronicles the continuance of prophecy in the earliest Christian communities; see especially his note on p. 145. For a discussion of the contemporary pastoral implications of prophecy, see "Prophetic Leadership Today" in our *The Promise of Partnership: A Model for Collaborative Ministry*.

In *Body and Society*, historian Peter Brown traces the effort to interpret Paul's convictions about "the flesh and the spirit" in the new cultural contexts of early Christianity. See, for example, his excellent discussions on pp. 48 and 418; Brown outlines Clement's stoic understanding of passion on p. 129. The quotations of Marcus Aurelius are taken from B.N.A. Grube's translation of *The Meditations*; see pp. 11, 46, 53, 96, and 118.

Josef Pieper explores the power of wrath, anger, and courage in *The Four Cardinal Virtues*. Lee Yearley discusses *ch'i* in relation to courage in *Mencius and Aquinas: Theories of Virtue and Conceptions of Courage*; see especially pp. 152 and following. Henry Fairlie's comment on anger is found in *The Seven Deadly Sins Today*, p. 87.

For Aristotle's discussion of anger, see *Nicomachean Ethics*, #1125b26–1126b10. Thomas Aquinas examines anger in Questions 46–48, in the first section of the second part (Ia–IIae) of the *Summa Theologiae*. Aquinas's optimistic interpretation of the passions appears in Question 59. There he carefully distinguishes two very different views of the passions: "If by passions we mean inordinate affections, as the Stoics held, then it is clear that perfect virtue is without passions. But if by passions we mean *all movements of sense appetite*, then it is plain that the moral virtues, which are about the passions as their proper matter, *cannot be without the passions*"; see p. 96 in *The Treatise on the Virtues*, translated by John Oesterle (our emphasis). This notion of virtues as bodily resources rather than purely spiritual strengths was alien to Augustine and much of early Christianity.

Alasdair MacIntyre examines the positive role of conflict in *After Virtue*, see pp. 160 and 206; on p. 153 MacIntyre quotes philosopher John Anderson on the revelatory role of conflict in society; on p. 179 MacIntyre explores the link between care and courage. MacIntyre examines the revolutionary potential of temperance in "*Sophrosunē*: How a Virtue Can Become Socially Disruptive."

11

Transforming Social Shame

"Do it this way," says shame, "or you'll be sorry."
Elizabeth Janeway

The puzzle of shame begins in the many meanings of the word. Shame names the discomfort we feel in the embarrassing moments of everyday life. But in some contexts shame carries a positive nuance: a healthy sense of shame alerts us to one another's vulnerability, adding delicacy and respect to our social interactions. The word functions in this sense, for example, when we say "Have you no shame!?" to accuse someone of acting without sensitivity or tact. And in the influential vocabulary of therapy and recovery, shame identifies a corrosive mood of personal inferiority that defeats all achievement and delight.

The American inclination toward individualism disposes us to interpret shame as a negative, private feeling. But even these most intimate awarenesses are shaped by social forces. The environments of family, religion, and nation orchestrate our embarrassments. Healing shame's damaging force requires a grasp of the social dynamics that shape this pervasive emotion.

The Economy of Shame: The Measure of Our Worth

Complex, shadowy rules govern the experience of social shame. To trace this economy, the human concern for *earning* and *paying* respect is a good place to start. Respect refers, literally, to how we are seen by others. Playing by society's rules, we hope to be seen in a favorable light. We earn respect by doing a good job at work, by meeting our commitments in friendship, by keeping our word. Eager to be well regarded ourselves, we show our respect for others. In childhood we learn the debt of respect we owe our elders. As adults, we gather at memorial services and funerals to pay our respects to the deceased and the survivors alike.

The economy of earning and paying respect inducts us into the world of respectability. Even as children we are keenly aware which homes in the neighborhood are respectable and which are not. We learn whether our own parents work within respected occupations. We sense the dictates of fashion—the class requirements of dress and demeanor, the special regard shown certain initials: M.D., BMW, C.E.O. We suffer the perils of this economy, as well, when shifts in fashion leave us painfully vulnerable. Our house, our wardrobe, even our body size may suddenly lose value and no longer merit respect.

In such an economy of scarcity, external evaluation measures our worth. When others approve of us, we feel appreciated: our value increases. But if others frown on our choice of friends or profession or leisure activities, our worth plummets. Our value depreciates, catapulting us into an emotional—if not economic—depression.

Like respect, honor is a social measure of our worth. And like respect, honor is embedded in an economy of scarcity. In the novel and film *Prizzi's Honor,* the threat of dishonor casts a constant shadow. Ever vigilant against the loss of honor, members of these close-knit mafia families live with the specter of revenge: violent retaliation is demanded to restore their diminished honor. The Spanish proverb says it clearly: "The stain of honor is washed clean in blood." Honor and shame are blood relatives.

Even in our own culture, seemingly free of the social code of honor and vengeance, the romance of revenge remains powerful. American honor sanctions violence in the service of injured dignity. Hollywood exalts this theme: In Clint Eastwood's award-winning film *Unforgiven,* retired killers return to their bloody profession to avenge an injury to a prostitute. Their honor, like the woman's, is at stake; moviegoers' response to the film's violent resolution confirms that revenge earns respect.

The romance of vengeance also helps legitimize war. The young are recruited to the task—and honor—of dying for their country. Military memorials and medals of honor seek to convince us that our soldiers do not die in vain. In vain: for vanity's sake; without purpose; in pursuit of the phantom of national honor. The honor of war still haunts our young nation decades after its defeat in Vietnam.

The economy of social shame is driven by an interminable search for respect and honor. Love is the antidote to this economy. Its unearned affection reminds us of another measure of our worth. Our parents' gratuitous care does not depend on what we can achieve. Blessed by the enduring affection of friends and companions, we feel our value soar. Being loved teaches us to calculate respect differently. If we are fortunate, we learn our inestimable value does not depend on status or possessions. Our worth is rooted in something more fundamental than social conformity.

Yet, being human, we fall prey to the social dynamics of shame. Our vulnerable desire for respect recruits us to dependence on society's constant approval. Every society takes advantage of this leverage to compel conformity. This brings us to the story of social shaming.

The Strategies of Social Shaming

The pain of shame reminds us that our behavior is in public view. People who matter to us are watching. If we measure up, we may be deemed acceptable—recognized as worthy to be "one of them." If these significant folk find our actions unacceptable, they may turn away their gaze. Now we risk being excluded—from their affection, from their protection, from the security of belonging to this elite group. As a psychological dynamic, then, shame seeks to insure inclusion. As a social strategy, shaming attempts to enforce conformity.

The family table teaches us the price of inclusion. There our parents curb our preference for eating with our hands! They praise us for using the knife and fork properly and scold us for playing with our food. They instruct us in the rigors of delayed gratification: dessert remains untouchable so long as vegetables linger on our plate. If we don't comply, we risk being sent from the room—"until you can show that you belong here with the rest the family."

These tasks of socialization—teaching table manners, encouraging potty training, urging us to share our toys—begin early. Parents start to shape behavior long before their infants and toddlers have a full range of cognitive skills. Before the appeal to rational persuasion can be effective, as we saw in Chapter 8, parents use other strategies in the service of socialization. Unilaterally, parents set the behavior standards to be met; they closely monitor the child's performance, rewarding achievement and discouraging resistance. Rules abound: "Don't cross the street by yourself"; "be sure to wash your hands before meals"; "let your little brother play with that toy." Motivation is simple: "Do as I say . . . because I say so." At this early developmental stage, conformity is the goal: Children's external behavior is more important—to their safety as well as their social acceptance—than is their agreement with the family rules in force.

As a strategy in group life, shaming outlasts infancy. Shame comes into play whenever external criteria are favored in evaluating personal experience. The threat of social shame conveys two messages: we will show you how to act here; you cannot survive apart from our approval and protection.

Social shame warns, "If you do not fit in, you will be cast out; worse, you make yourself an outcast." Recognition and respect (it argues) are gifts of membership, benefits of belonging to the group. To be deprived of the community's resources and affirmation is to be disgraced. Literature and history are rife with instances of this shaming. An officer of the French Foreign Legion has his insignia stripped off his uniform; a woman accused of a sexual offense is clothed with a scarlet letter; former preacher Jim Bakker is led to jail in leg irons, not because he is a flight risk, but to make his disgrace evident to all. While shaming supports human development during that short season before we are equipped for responsibility and conscience, its adult forms are almost always destructive.

Shaming and Naming

A chief strategy of social shame is to name a person as deviant. Names tell us who we are, assigning both identity and worth. When a beleaguered parent, discovering that a four-year-old has wet the bed again, scolds "bad girl!", the child hears herself identified negatively for something she could not control. With the taunt of "chicken, chicken," youngsters dare the new kid on the block to throw a stone at a street lamp. Intimidated by the chant and desperate to dispel its punishing claim, the child acts against his better judgment.

Deviant names stigmatize, marking the shamed person as not fitting in, as unworthy of membership in this group. This labeling strategy survives in our religious and political lives. Threatened by the assertive behavior of a woman new to the management team, the old-timers label her a *bitch*. Eager to avoid this degrading title, she may decide to adopt a more docile attitude; the shaming strategy has worked.

Americans are especially vicious in sexual and gender slurs. Names like *pervert*, *fag*, *dyke*, and *queer* stigmatize those whose sexual behavior hints they are not "one of us." And the strategy of this naming may take a more subtle and violent turn. In the summer of 1992 a Vatican document arrived on the desks of U.S. Catholic bishops. The text instructed these religious leaders to resist pending legislation to prevent discrimination against gay and lesbian citizens in housing and employment. The curious logic of the document acknowledged that all persons enjoy the right to housing and employment, but argued that these rights could be "legitimately limited" in certain situations—as, for example, in "the case of contagious or mentally ill persons." The authors of the document would no doubt insist that these are simply examples. But the ordinary reader associates "contagious or mentally ill persons" with the focus of the text: homosexuals. Such a strategy of shaming is especially destructive when cloaked as religious instruction.

Naming as deviant—whether the bed-wetter or the assertive woman or the homosexual—serves two intentions: to expose the person and to threaten expulsion from the group. A derogatory name singles us out. Most of us have grammar school memories of being asked to stand up in class or come to the front of the room. We cringed at the thought of this sudden exposure. What if we are asked something we don't know? What if the teacher decides to make an example of us? Behind this threat of exposure is the unspoken lesson: hidden within the group, we are safe. By fitting in and acting as others do, we avoid the embarrassment of exposure.

The dynamic of social shaming takes advantage of our enduring vulnerability. At the taunt of *chicken*, whether we are seven or forty-seven, we wonder: "Am I really afraid to try something new and bold?" Recoiling at the sound of *bitch*, we question our own strength: "Perhaps I did come on too strong at the meeting; I'll have to watch myself next time." Assaulted again by the jeers of *dyke* or *fag*, we return to doubts we thought had been resolved: "Is it okay to be who I am? If not, who shall I be?"

If naming exposes us, it also threatens expulsion. Called to the front of the class, we stand close to the door, in jeopardy of being sent away. Every group develops exquisite tools to threaten its members with expulsion. We tell our child to leave the table until she can behave like the others. We send another child to his room until he learns how to behave. The threat's power lies not in actual banishment; note that the children are still in the house. But their belonging is now in jeopardy.

Within some Amish communities, a person who significantly offends against the group's rules is shunned by other members. Again, the offender is not driven away but is instead threatened with psychological abandonment. Hidden in the threat of expulsion is the conviction that individuals cannot survive apart from the group. Perhaps this fear is rooted in millennia of survival in hostile climates where, deprived of the community's food and fire, the isolated individual would certainly perish. For several centuries Christian piety professed that "outside the church there is no salvation." Those separated from this saving community were doomed to eternal punishment; fire of another sort.

Belittling and Belonging

Social shame's second strategy is belittling. "You're such a cry baby!" we rebuke the youngster who is frightened by the dark. Calling the child immature, we hope to shame him into acting more adult, more "like us."

Ignoring and forgetting are other forms of belittling. Remember the day the teacher or camp director called the list of names and omitted yours? Suddenly you felt yourself diminished; in this important person's mind, you did not exist. Or in gym class when sides were chosen for the game, and you were left standing on the sidelines, abandoned and belittled.

Belittling aims to reawaken whatever woundedness we still carry from childhood: memories of being left out or overlooked, fears of being forgotten. When it can evoke the trauma of abandonment, the strategy of belittling gains enormous power.

In civic and religious life, belittling reappears in efforts to trivialize a cherished concern. The question of sexist language in the liturgy—constant references to "brothers" and "all men" that suggest God's people come only in one gender—is declared by some leaders to be insignificant. The message: You should be ashamed of making so much of this unimportant matter. Raising a fuss here is just silly.

Laughter sometimes belittles. Humor, of course, plays many roles in group life. Laughing at our mistakes and poking fun at our worries reduces social tension. But humor is easily recruited as a weapon to keep others in their place: We make fun of people to "put them down," to expose them as inferior to ourselves.

In the service of shame, humor turns to ridicule. We laugh at those foolish enough to try for a job that doesn't "fit" her ethnic background or his class. "They should have known better. Who do they think they are!" Here laughter hardly hides the hostility. And humor, steeped in bitterness, becomes scorn. In the late stages of the 1992 presidential campaign George Bush played out a final and futile card of social shame, mocking his opponent as "the failed governor of a small state."

Shaming by Silencing

Silencing, like belittling, hopes to diminish a threat to the group's good order. Rather than instigating a dialogue to clear the air, silencing aims to quiet the voice that dissents. Exasperated parents shout at the troublesome child, "shut up!" Irritated religious officials impose periods of silence on dissenting theologians. The intent here, as in all strategies of social shame, is to reinforce self-doubt. During this penitential silence, the offending parties will learn to modify their tone. And others tempted to speak out of turn will be forewarned and forestalled.

Better understanding this strategy of social shame may illumine the pressures experienced by young women socialized in American culture. Provocative studies by feminist psychologists suggest that powerful social forces silence young women at critical moments in their development. Carol Gilligan and her colleagues have documented a trend for girls to "lose their voice" in their early teen years. Once boisterous risk-takers, these young women shrink into docile compliance. The mid-life woman in Alice Munro's short story "Open Secrets" recalls this diminishment in her own life:

> She remembered how noisy she had been then. A shrieker, a dare-taker. Just before she hit high school a giddiness either genuine or faked or half -and-half became available to her. Soon it vanished, her bold body vanished inside this ample one, and she became a studious, shy girl, a blusher. She developed the qualities her husband would see and value when hiring and proposing. . . . To be careless, dauntless, to create havoc—that is the lost hope of girls.

The factors that strangle initiative and will in the service of social conformity cannot be far from shame. Uncovering these still hidden dynamics of adolescent socialization will help liberate girls and women alike.

The Transformation of Social Shame

Healing shame depends on the development of personal antidotes to these social strategies. Learning to trust our own instincts will attune us to the difference between personal goals and social conventions. Reinterpreting risk, we can embrace failure not as a shameful sign of personal inadequacy but as an acceptable scene in the drama of our vocation.

Cultivating the strength of will offers another antidote. Learning to be assertive helps us develop a flexible sense of boundaries—where we leave off and another person begins, where our rights intersect with those of others, where personal hopes put us in tension with people significant to us. Negotiating these interpersonal boundaries, we each craft our own balance of intimacy and solitude, of merger and independence. Gradually coming to trust our own instincts and to rely on our sense of boundaries leaves us less a prey to the forces of social shame.

An effective challenge to social shame takes more than individual discipline. Shaming strategies draw energy from deep cultural roots, the hidden assumptions and unspoken rules that govern our common life. Who is in and who is out? What shade of skin, what level of income, what beliefs and behavior are required to be included? Do outsiders have access to our bounty? Who has a right to belong? Invalidating the destructive strategies of social shame demands transforming these images of belonging. And in this social transformation of shame, religion can become an important ally.

Religion plays a highly ambiguous role in the realm of shame and belonging. Religious institutions have long employed shame and guilt to threaten their members. For many adults, religion's chief heritage has been a burden of shame around sexuality. Garrison Keillor's character in *Lake Wobegon Days* speaks for many Christians as he describes a religious upbringing with bitter humor:

> You have taught me to feel shame and disgust about my body, so that I am afraid to clear my throat or blow my nose. . . . You

taught me an indecent fear of sexuality. I'm not sure I have any left underneath this baked-on crust of shame and disgust. . . . A year ago a friend offered to give me a backrub. I declined vociferously. You did this to me.

Despite its history of malpractice, Christianity can make a powerful contribution to the healing of social shame.

Christianity and the Healing of Social Shame

Religion, as a purifying force within human culture, invites us to reexamine our suppositions about social status and worth. As a society narrows its rules for who is included and who is highly regarded, religion challenges us to reform our criteria for inclusion and esteem. Religion's best contribution to the healing of social shame may be in undermining the conventional rules of belonging.

The prophets reminded ancient Israel that widows and orphans and the poor were not outcasts, but members of the community. Yahweh's covenant with Israel had redefined the social indicators of status and worth. Because they were beloved by a compassionate God, the prophets insisted, these people are part of our family.

In the Christian gospel, Jesus continues this critique of the human inclination to exclude the lowly and the marginal from the community. When he is told that members of his family had arrived to visit him, Jesus' response startles his tight-knit group of followers: "Who is my mother and who are my brothers?" (Matt. 12:48). Then, following the lead of the ancient prophets, he redraws the boundaries of belonging: "Whoever does the will of my father in heaven is my brother and sister and mother." In a single stroke, Jesus overturns the authority of traditional clan lines. The centrality of ethnic kinship, with its ancient grudges and sensitivity to dishonor, is thrown into doubt. The concern for blood lines, with its vigilance around shame and justification of revenge, comes into question.

Five times in Matthew's gospel, Jesus challenges these "family values." The ancient commandment to "honor thy parents" is now balanced by the need to leave them, in order to follow Jesus (See Matt. 4:22; 8:22; 19:29). At his most antagonistic, Jesus warns his followers that he has not "come to bring peace, but a sword. For I have come to set a man against his father, and a daughter against her mother . . ."

(Matt. 10:34–35). Christians have often preferred to ignore this questioning of family values that would compel us to welcome every kind of outcast into our midst.

When religion redraws the boundaries of belonging, it alters the criteria of our worth and our dignity. Reading the Jewish prophets or the life of Jesus, we momentarily glimpse the truth we find hard to embrace: A person's value is not rooted in his group's social status or her family's pride of place. Our worth springs neither from the superiority of our clan nor from our personal righteousness. Our value and dignity arise from our inalienable bond to a Creator who judges that all creation is "very good."

This shift in the measure of our worth—from social status, civic pride, and moral rectitude to God's unconditional love—opens a novel remedy for social transgressions. When our dignity balances on the fragile respectability of our kin, we will be ever anxious to avenge injuries. Apprehensive about losing respect, we ready ourselves for the ancient remedy. In a group dominated by a concern for its status and worth, vengeance prowls the borders of our belonging; any insult to our honor triggers the instinct for revenge. Neighborhood arguments, fights between gangs, wars between nations mushroom in our endless quest for respect.

But if our belonging is anchored in a more powerful source of worth, another remedy is available: instead of vengeance, forgiveness. In place of an unending retaliation for injuries received, we can break this cycle with a novel and surprising act of reconciliation. We can surrender the obsessive pursuit of social respect and learn to give and receive pardon. This extraordinary gesture must appear foolish to the wise of the world. And to those still injured by a personal history of shame, forgiveness may seem intolerable, looking like more of the same passivity before others' intrusions and abuse. But forgiveness remains a possibility. When we are blessed with the ability to forgive, we feel the corrosive demands of shame and vengeance begin to dissolve. In their place is revealed a common humanity, both blessed and broken—the better measure of our worth.

Shame and Seeing Face to Face

Shame is both about belonging and being seen: how we are regarded by others. At the beginning of Christianity looms the shameful public execution of a naked Jesus. This startling memory must indicate a special contribution of Christianity to the healing of social shame. The story of the Christian transformation of shame unfolds in three acts. In act one, a couple wanders through an idyllic garden, "naked and unashamed" (Gen. 2:25). Once upon a time, our religious memory tells us, we were fully exposed to one another and were not embarrassed. Adam and Eve lived, without protection or apology, face-to-face with God. But once they disobeyed their Creator, they felt suddenly exposed and rushed to cover themselves. Dis-covered by the eyes of God, they were asked the fateful question: "Who told you you were naked?" Henceforth, humans would need to protect their acute sense of shame with clothing and would have to shield themselves from direct contact with their Creator.

Act two begins at this moment and continues through the Hebrew Scriptures. For the ancient Israelites and many other religious traditions, the *sacred* was recognized as dangerous terrain. God's special haunts—whether on a holy mountain or in a temple sanctuary—must be marked off with special barriers. Humans must not come too close to this awesome and potentially lethal power. Moses is warned to "mark off the limits of the mountain and declare it sacred" (Exod. 19:23, (JB)) and that "whoever touches the mountain will be put to death" (Exod. 19:12, (JB)).

On Mount Sinai Moses pleads to see God's face, but is told, "You cannot see my face, for a human cannot see me and live" (Exod. 33:20, JB). (Elsewhere another tradition suggested a greater intimacy between Yahweh and Moses: When Moses would enter the Tent of Visitation in their desert encampment, "Yahweh would speak with Moses *face to face*, as a person speaks with his friend" [Exod. 33:11, JB].) Humans learned to cover their faces and shield their eyes in the presence of God. This separation of the sacred and the human was ritualized in the curtain that enshrouded the Holy of Holies in the temple in Jerusalem, shielding human eyes from God's direct gaze. The altar railing in many Christian churches lingers as a vestige of this conviction that sacred space must be marked off from ordinary secular territory.

During this long second act, humankind learned reverence for a mysterious and powerful God; coming before God they bowed their heads, lowered their voice, bent their knee. A healthy sense of shame alerted believers to the vulnerable boundary that both links us to and separates us from God. Like Adam and Eve, we became acutely aware in God's presence and covered ourselves with reverential behavior.

Act three: The death of Jesus Christ erupts with revolutionary force into this long religious tradition of shame and reverence. Jesus suffers a humiliating public death. He is tortured and exposed and ridiculed. But, as the New Testament observes, "Jesus . . . endured the cross, *disregarding* its shame" (Heb. 12:2) [emphasis added]. The public shaming of his death did not humiliate him; he did not cast his eyes down in embarrassment nor dissolve in despair. He faced his death without losing face.

In his death the Christian story of shame mysteriously comes full circle: Jesus is naked and unashamed. But now the exposure is not the romantic nakedness of the primeval garden, but the degrading exposure of a public execution. Yet the humiliating circumstances of this death did not humiliate Jesus: he disregarded the shamefulness of the cross. Embracing his death, Jesus transforms the power of social shame. Christians celebrate this transformation in their devotion to the crucifix; what at first seems to be a shameful failure, to be concealed in embarrassment, is raised up as a sign of suffering that has been healed.

The way that Jesus dies, the manner and dignity with which he embraces his end, saps death of its absurdity and its sting. The pain of death is not magically removed, but its degradation and humiliation are lifted. Because he has died this way, every other death becomes more tolerable, less absurd. But the mysterious transformation his death provides extends beyond physical death to every traumatic experience of shame. Christians who have suffered severe abuse in childhood bring their shame to prayer and religious liturgy. There they encounter someone who has survived profound social shame—Jesus who has been humbled without being destroyed. Though ridiculed, his worth has not been squandered. Though exposed in all his vulnerability, he has not been found inferior. Rejected by society, he has been embraced by God. This extraordinary event encourages Christians to dare expose their hidden shame to the Lord and feel its power dissolve.

In the account of Jesus' death in Matthew's gospel, we are told that "the veil of the Temple was torn in two from top to bottom. . ." (Matt. 27:51). The barrier and covering between the sacred and the human, so necessary since our expulsion from the garden, is removed. This sudden revelation of the sacred echoes the exposure of Jesus' body on the cross. The hidden is revealed and the secret made public. An ancient religious arrangement has come to an end, and with it the rules for public shame.

The author of the Letter to the Hebrews interprets the tearing of the veil: "We have confidence to enter the sanctuary by the blood of Jesus, by the new and living way he has opened for us through the curtain (that is, through his flesh)" . . . (Heb. 10:19). The message is the revolutionary gift of the Incarnation: In Jesus we see God in the flesh, we meet God face to face. The traditionally necessary boundaries protecting us from God's awesome presence are removed.

We find a clue to the transforming power of Jesus' death in a similar fate recorded in the beautiful poetry of the Book of Isaiah. "A suffering servant" suffers a death that is surrounded by social shame:

> He was despised and rejected by others,
> A man of suffering and acquainted with infirmity.
> And as one from whom others hid their faces.
> He was despised and we held him of no account.
>
> *Isa. 53:3*

But then the poet suggests the mysterious power of this suffering: "Surely he has borne our infirmities and carried our diseases . . . upon him was the punishment that made us whole, and by his bruises we are healed" (Isa. 53:4–5).

What do Christians mean when we say of the suffering servant, "by his bruises we are healed"? Seeing Jesus face his death with courage and integrity powerfully affects us. When we observe that he is not humiliated by the shameful circumstance of his suffering, we wonder if we need be so ashamed of our pain. His disregarding of the shamefulness of his death encourages us to see our shame differently, to begin to question the need to conceal and hide our woundedness. Perhaps we too can expose our shame to God, to a counselor or close friend. When we are so empowered, shame loses its control over us. We begin to disregard the shamefulness of our own injuries and can say, "by his bruises we are healed."

The success of social shaming insures its survival. Threats of ridicule or rejection will continue to enforce conformity and guarantee compliance. But other resources, companions of psychological maturing and religious faith, can equip us to explore alternate measures of our worth. Our Christian heritage, despite its frequent complicity in social shaming, offers us opportunities to redefine belonging, to convert our thirst for vengeance into a willingness to forgive, and to heal our shame.

Reflective Exercise

All of us have experienced social shaming; many of us have used shaming as a strategy ourselves. Begin this reflection by recalling a recent occasion when some technique of social shaming was used against you. The setting may have been your work site, your extended family, the civic community, or the church.

First, identify the shaming strategies involved: were you belittled or excluded or silenced or mocked or . . . ? Give examples to show concretely what was involved.

Then, consider how these shaming techniques affected you. Can you recall the threat you felt? How did you respond; what were your thoughts, emotions, actions? What resources helped you deal with or resist this effort to shame you?

Finally, in what ways has your religious experience been a help in your efforts to heal the effects of social shaming? In what ways has it been a hindrance?

Additional Resources

Elizabeth Janeway offers wise and provocative counsel for dealing with social dynamics of shaming in *Improper Behavior: When and How Misconduct Can Be Healthy for Society*. In *Vital Involvement in Old Age: The Experience of Old Age in Our Time*, Erik Erikson, Joan M. Erikson, and Helen Q. Kivnick trace connections between early personal experiences of shame and later life experience. Donald L. Nathanson undertakes a broad synthesis of current research perspectives on shame in its social contexts in *Shame and Pride: Affect, Sex, and the Birth of the Self*; see also his earlier *The Many Faces of Shame*.

In *God With Us: The Trinity and Christian Life*, Catherine Mowry LaCugna explores the Trinity in terms of God's presence to humankind, instead of a more traditional God-in-Godself series of relationships apart from creation; see also Mary Aquin O'Neill's discussion of "The Mystery of Being Human Together" in *Freeing Theology: The Essentials of Theology in Feminist Perspective*, edited by Catherine Mowry La-

Cugna. Carl Schneider speaks suggestively of the significance of Jesus' death for the transformation of shame in *Shame, Exposure and Privacy*; see p. 115. We examine the elusive interplay of scarcity and abundance in *The Promise of Partnership: A Model for Collaborative Ministry*.

Carol Gilligan and her colleagues continue the pioneering investigation of women's experience begun in her influential book *In a Different Voice*. For incisive analyses of the social dynamics that undermine confidence among adolescent girls, see *Making Connections: The Relational Worlds of Adolescent Girls*, edited by C. Gilligan, N. Lyons, and T. Hammer and *Meeting at the Crossroads: Women's Psychology and Girl's Development*, by Lyn Mikel Brown and Carol Gilligan. Alice Munro's short story "Open Secrets" appeared in the *New Yorker* magazine, February 8, 1993; we quote from p. 93. Garrison Keillor's observations on shame appear in *Lake Wobegon Days*, pp. 254, 257, 259.

For an example of silencing used as a strategy within the religious community, see the 1986 article "L'Affaire Curran" by Richard McCormick and the 1990 article "L'Affaire Curran II" by Richard McCormick and Richard McBrien, both of which appeared in the journal *America*. Charles Curran describes this experience himself in *Faithful Dissent*. The statement urging American bishops to resist legislation which opposed housing discrimination against gays and lesbians appears in *Origins* (August 6, 1992), Vol. 22, #10 with an accompanying statement by Vatican spokesperson Joaquin Navarro-Valls.

12

Healing Depression: Giving Pain a Voice

Since I have lost all taste for life,
I will give free rein to my complaints;
I shall let my embittered soul speak out.
Job (JB)

The word *depression* embraces a range of experiences. An unresolved argument with a friend generates a disappointment that endures for days. Once the excitement of completing a challenging study program or finishing a long project passes, a heaviness of spirit dogs us for several months. Most of us learn to endure these "ambulatory" depressions without too much distress, recognizing the feelings as normal even if unpleasant. But then there are the mortal attacks. A woman regularly feels inundated by a paralyzing sadness that lasts weeks at a time; she's at a loss to explain why. Exhausted and bewildered, a talented teenager experiences difficulty with sleeping and loses interest in activities she previously enjoyed. A middle-aged man, feeling drained of energy and hope, senses his life grinding to a halt. Even more frightening to him, for the first time in his life he has contemplated suicide.

Depression has reached epidemic proportions in the United States. The National Institute of Mental Health estimates that fifteen million Americans each year suffer its afflictions. The causes of this affective disorder remain unclear. Medical analysis of family histories suggests a genetic disposition makes some of us especially susceptible. The success of antidepressant drugs like Lithium and Prozac underscores the links between body chemistry and this crippling mood. Still, most mental health professionals judge that drugs alone do not dissolve depression. But by lifting the mood, appropriate medication gives people the breathing space to examine the psychosocial forces that may be fueling their distress.

Confusing symptoms make diagnosing depression difficult. Moralistic attitudes make the diagnosis burdensome. Forty percent of Americans judge that depression is a sign of personal weakness; the remedy they advise is simply to "snap out of it." Associating depression with moral weakness, some people hesitate to seek treatment. Others couch their complaint as a physical ailment, seeking help for the more acceptable symptoms of insomnia or headache or fatigue.

The American temperament is upbeat. Members of a relatively young and prosperous nation, we endorse a naive optimism: "Don't worry; be happy!" Being caught up in grief or sadness seems somehow unpatriotic. But a deeper wisdom reminds us that every emotion deserves respect. Acknowledging what we are feeling is not the same as giving ourselves over to self-pity or despair. In a season of loss, in the face of disappointment, it's fitting that we be affected. Our survival depends on being in touch with what is happening around us. So when times are depressing, we should feel depressed.

How to decipher the bewildering experience of depression is the focus of this chapter. The initial conviction that guides our reflection is that depression is a social passion: more than an intrapsychic distress or sign of personal weakness, these painful feelings alert us to significant changes in our environment. Second, we will examine the everyday experiences of this mood rather than more traumatic episodes of clinical depression. Third, we will explore how depression, like the other negative emotions, begins as a healthy warning signal and only later spirals into a destructive mood.

A Self-Imposed Purge

Four years ago, Dillon remembers, he had really enjoyed his work. Now repetition and boredom meet him every day at the office. Getting up each morning is a chore. He gets frequent headaches and cannot seem to concentrate for long. Friends remark his usual cheerfulness is gone; he knows his confidence has vanished.

Sherry, recently divorced, moved to a new city last month. Despite the distractions of a new workplace and the comfort of a better climate, she is frequently sad. Throwing herself into her work, she fights off the feeling—for a time. But the malaise spreads, taking over more of her day. She spends more time watching television, snacks more often, finds meeting new friends difficult. Her sadness gradually deepens into the debilitating mood of despair.

Depression always seems to surprise us. Lethargy steals over us like a dense fog; misery settles in. This is no ordinary bad mood; Maggie Scarf calls depression a hybrid emotion, spawned by other intolerable feelings. But where did it come from? Why is it happening to us? What is it trying to say?

Philosopher Robert Solomon suggests that depression functions as "a self-imposed purge." Like other negative emotions, depression notifies us of something gone wrong. It comes, in Solomon's words, "to shake oneself loose from the archaic and outmoded sludge of encrusted tasks and values which one now finds worthless." When part of our life becomes unbearable, the symptoms of depression deliver the bad news. But the bad news is also good news: in Solomon's judgment, a depression can be "the beginning of self-realization, unless it is simply ignored, or drugged away, or allows itself to give in to the demands for its own avoidance—the most extreme of which is suicide."

By distinguishing *healthy* and *unhealthy* depression, psychologist Ellen McGrath makes clearer how depression can come as an ally. Like Solomon, she argues that depression's pain alerts us to a conflict that must be faced. In *When Feeling Bad Is Good*, McGrath reports the findings of a national study of depression in women commissioned by the American Psychological Association. The APA research found that many depressions are "cultural in origin" and "reasonably based on the events contributing to them." For example, an internalized cultural conscience holds most women accountable to external standards of appropriate feminine behavior. (Recall McGrath's list of the "Ten Commandments for Women" that we discussed in chapter 6.) Women who experience their own lives at odds with these cultural standards often become depressed. This kind of depression turns out to be healthy for many women, when it compels them to make decisions and undertake actions grounded in their own values.

British psychologist D.W. Winnicott follows a parallel path when he interprets depression as an "internal reassessment." The ability to reassess our life in the midst of a depression—rather than to simply succumb to the negative mood—is, for Winnicott, "an achievement of emotional growth." So depression makes us miserable, to be sure. But as Winnicott, McGrath, and Solomon insist, its symptoms are meant to be signals showing the way to healing and growth.

Seen in this optimistic light, depression may be more than a private disaster, more than a sign of personal weakness. This pain may be, in Solomon's words, one of "our most sophisticated and most radical means to shuffling the structures of our lives when they have become intolerable and unlivable." Our negative mood may function, paradoxically, as a positive strategy, urging us to see "through the values and structures which we have uncritically accepted and imposed upon ourselves, which we now find tedious, unlivable, and self-degrading." At heart, depression may be an invitation to grieve.

A depression descends on us with a mixed message: It leaves us feeling powerless at the same time it impels us to act. Like a nightmare, a depression both shows us ourself and shields us from some painful truth. Partially hidden in the disruption of a depression is a part of our life that needs attention. But, like a dream, this mood conceals as much as it reveals. So we wonder: Why do we feel this bad? Seeing our bad mood as only about ourself—our weakness, our inadequacy— tempts us to search out private solutions. We plunge more energetically into work or turn to the rapid remedies of alcohol or drugs—anything that might sedate the embarrassing distress. Private solutions for private pain. Poet Donald Hall describes that temptation in his own life: "Self-medication by alcohol gave temporary relief, brief lethal holiday and foretaste of death."

From Purge to Punishment

Because the symptoms of a depression both confuse and humiliate us, we are tempted to ignore them. When we do this, an opportunity passes. Ordinary depression settles into a chronic disorder. Freud described this destructive transition: The symptoms of a depression "proceed from a mental constellation of revolt, which has then, by a certain process, passed over into the crushed state of melancholia." From revolt to melancholy: The self-imposed purge becomes a long-term punishment.

Ellen McGrath traces depression's deterioration from healthy to unhealthy. Healthy depression alerts us to a conflict or loss that must be faced. In healthy depression our despondency comes and goes, leaving us still able to function. But by denying these painful signals or refusing to respond, we risk our depression deepening into an unhealthy mood disorder. Unhealthy depression cripples our ability to work and love. In the category of unhealthy depression McGrath includes those severe and lasting mood disorders that may well be biologically rooted. Whether genetically based or psychologically provoked (and this controversy still rages), severe depression is often life-threatening and requires professional assistance and appropriate medication.

Psychologist David Burns, an advocate of cognitive therapy, finds depression's roots in distorted thinking. People susceptible to depression have *learned to interpret* their experience in self-defeating ways. Arriving late for an important appointment, for example, we castigate ourself with messages like "I'm always late!" or "Why can't I do anything right?" Catching ourselves in a simple mistake, we magnify the experience: "I'm such a loser!" These interpretive distortions engender depression, especially when they regularly haunt our inner dialogue. Healing begins in tracking our own self-talk, recognizing that we can *unlearn* these punishing patterns. The approach of cognitive therapy strikes some therapists as a bit too rational, but many people struggling with simple depression praise its success. For those caught in the vortex of self-criticism, Burns's practical focus on the inner conversation shows a way out.

Maggie Scarf defines depression as "a failure in adaptation; an inability to cope, at some juncture, with the ongoing inner and outer shifts and changes which each of us must confront throughout our human existence." Scarf judges that "anxiety is an important survival mechanism," because when we are anxious we are still struggling with our problems. "Depression is, contrariwise, a state of 'after the battle is over.' It has been likened to defeat at the end of the war, to desolation, to a state of having given in and given up."

Depression's characteristic symptom, Scarf notes, is "the inability to experience pleasure . . . ; to be depressed is to be thoroughly incapable of enjoying one's life." A depressed person loses the ability to enjoy a fine meal or conversation with a good friend. Weighed down by depression, he fears he must be a dreadful companion—and than acts like one. "The mood state is itself a filter of experience, allowing nothing cheerful or gratifying to come through." Counselors suggest that depressed people judge they are *unworthy* of delight. A child's success in school, a beautiful spring day, a promotion at work—when we are depressed none of these can penetrate the screen that blocks out pleasure, pleasure we have decided we do not deserve.

In *Unfinished Business: Pressure Points in the Lives of Women*, Scarf gives special attention to women's difficulty with separation. Often, her research suggests, a woman will feel distressed about a relationship—with parents or spouse or friend—that she sees as indispensable. She dares not risk upsetting this relationship, so she internalizes the distress. She blames herself for the problem, rather than face the conflict entailed in confronting the other person. Directing her anger and guilt at herself, she becomes depressed. "Becoming depressed is a way of discharging those awful, negative feelings; and yet leaving the needed emotional bond intact." By feeling this bad, she punishes herself (which seems appropriate, since she feels guilty) while guaranteeing that the relationship will not to jeopardized. It is, as Scarf concludes, "a very bad bargain."

Taking Scarf's emphasis on women's difficulty with separation as a point of departure, Dana Crowley Jack argues that depression arises from difficulties with *sustaining* healthy, secure attachments. A culture of inequality tells women that dependence and attachment are signs of weakness. The cultural (and masculine) ideal of the separate self favors autonomy over interdependence. When a woman feels the healthy need to be deeply connected with others, she is likely to judge this longing as a sign of inadequacy. If she were stronger, she tells herself, she would not be so "dependent." Feeling inadequate and inferior, she blames herself and slips into a depression.

Depression arises in the lives of women not because of a loss of a relationship with parent or spouse or child but because of *the loss of herself* within a relationship. A woman sustains the relationship, as Jack demonstrates in *Silencing the Self*, but at the price of her own integrity. The cultural script for "a good wife" exemplifies this dilemma. Many women are socialized to see their primary role as supporting their spouse. The husband's role as provider requires his focus outside the home, effectively exempting men from reciprocal, emotional contributions on the domestic front. To achieve the "good wife" goal, a woman must stifle conflict, silence anger, and postpone her own needs and dreams. Over time this neglect of self erodes her sense of self-worth. In Jesse Bernard's poignant phrase, she "diminishes into a wife." Witnessing themselves shrinking into the wifely role, recognizing their own collusion in the process, and sensing no real alternatives are available, traps many women in a spiral of self-loathing and despair. This cultural dynamic, insists Dana Crowley Jack, is the real source of the epidemic of women's depression today.

Giving Our Pain a Voice

Embarrassed by depression and ignorant of its origins, we are tempted to withdraw from others and privatize our pain. These temptations hide the clues for healing this destructive mood.

Three thousand years ago our religious ancestors modeled a different method for dealing with depression. In a time of disaster or confusion they would lift up their voices in complaint. Refusing to collapse into private sadness, they gave public expression to their pain. The Book of Lamentations records their distress:

> All you who pass this way, look and see:
> Is any sorrow like the sorrow that afflicts me,
> With which Yahweh has struck me
> On the day of his burning anger?
>
> Lam. 1:12 (JB)

Stricken by grief, our ancestors refused the silence of depression. They gave voice to their pain. The poetry of the Psalms turns repeatedly to this theme:

> I am worn out with groaning,
> Every night I drench my pillow
> And soak my bed with tears;
> My eye is wasted with grief,
> I have grown old with enemies all around me.
>
> Ps. 6:6 (JB)

The lamentation of the ancient Hebrews was a noisy, rancorous style of prayer. Their loud and persistent groans were a strategy to get God's attention; reproaching their Creator they demanded explanation of their pain. In Job's words, "I shall say to God, 'do not condemn me, but tell me the reason for your assault'" (Job 10:2, JB). As scripture scholar Walter Brueggemann observes, in their laments the prophets believed "that the daring speech of earth, when done with passion and shrillness, can change the affairs of heaven." We do not know how this works, of course; somehow, "it is pain brought to speech and made available in the community that is the mediator of new life."

Publicizing Our Pain

To heal our hurt, we will have to find a voice for our distress. A family finds itself in a crisis. The parents rarely speak with each other; a teenage daughter has become anorexic; a son is angry and uncooperative. For months the family sullenly trudges through its daily interactions, pretending before neighbors and relatives that "all is well."

Finally, by some grace or good fortune, the family seeks help. With a counselor's assistance, family members begin to speak to one another. At first, their situation together becomes much worse. Previously buried distress now boils over, scalding each and all. But with skillful guidance, they learn to give names to their animosities without mortally injuring each other. Acknowledging patterns of behavior that simply don't work, they search together for new ways to relate. Slowly, by voicing their pain and lamenting their wounds, the family begins to mend.

Sharing our distress changes our ways of being together; we heal both our souls and our society. From the time of slavery, African Americans have given voice to their pain in song. In their music, a people afflicted by exploitation and hardship intoned their grief. Now part of the heritage of their rich contribution to American culture, "singing the blues" continues to work its healing effect. The transforming magic of melody and rhythm makes pain more bearable. By turning private pain into public song, the blues soothe people's distress and salve depression into grief. In chapter 2 we recounted William Stringfellow's distinction of grief as the first experience of loss and mourning as "the liturgies of recollection" by which we turn our pain into prayer. In our use of the term, *grief* stands for the entire process of acknowledging our pain and facing our loss.

The transformation of private depression into shared grief takes place daily at the Vietnam Memorial in our nation's capital. Even as troops withdrew from the small battle-scarred country of Vietnam, most Americans refused to admit a national failure. Surely we had not lost the war; what our retreat achieved, we insisted, was peace with honor.

Yet veterans came home to encounter anger or silence, as the country tried to put the experience behind us and move on. As a nation we hoped that if we ignored our negative emotions, they would disappear. But they did not. Disillusionment settled over the country at large; veterans exhibited surprising psychological symptoms; politicians postured to the world that "America is still strong."

Then the U.S. Congress commissioned the construction of a national memorial of the Vietnam conflict, modeled on a design submitted by an Asian American woman. Turning away from the tradition of heroic figures bristling with weapons, artist Maya Lin incised into a small hillock a black wall of names. The stone glistened like a scar in the earth, beckoning visitors as though to an entry into a crypt. Daily now, Americans come to search out the names of friends and relatives. Then they reach out to touch, as though the name was etched in braille. Tears are released for both private and public losses. A natural silence surrounds the site, as if to protect our private grief. But we come to this wall together and perform our common ritual in public. Television coverage magnifies the mourning, allowing an entire nation to join its sorrow in these somber rites of recognition. At this wall, the nation prays its lament and honors its communal debt of grief.

Another symbolic action has released a second national mourning. The shame associated with the disease AIDS had prompted us, as a people, to keep the earliest deaths secret. We agreed that our colleague had died from cancer or pneumonia. We conspired to privatize our pain. Then, quite suddenly, the quilt appeared. Patches of colored material were joined together and exhibited for public viewing. Individual lives, rescued from anonymous death, were stitched together into one broad, comforting fabric. Viewers walked slowly from section to section, acknowledging the enormity of our common loss. The genius of the symbol guaranteed its effect: a warm, protective blanket comforting us even as it allowed us to grieve the lives woven on its cloth.

Americans, with our love for practical remedies, continue to create self-help groups that provide oases of grieving in an anonymous society. Alcoholics Anonymous presents a simple, nonhierarchical structure in which participants can acknowledge failure and regret and ask for support. The group encourages laments but not excuses, and the dynamic of voicing one's distress rescues the recovering alcoholic from the secret, destructive habits that feed a depression. Similar organizations have mushroomed over the past several decades. Mothers Against Drunk Driving, the group we mentioned in chapter 4, is a thoroughly American expression of productive lamentation. Enraged over the death of children in alcohol-related accidents, these women refused to simply turn their grief inward in guilt and depression. Instead they organize effective lobbying efforts for laws punishing those who drink and drive. Their gatherings provide both a place of support in a time of loss, and a means to channel energy in constructive directions.

Anti-rape activist Barbara Engel leads discussions that link the private pain of rape survivors with a social consciousness about sexual violence. Often the trauma of the abuse isolates these women. When they fall silent and withdraw, their witness is lost to a society afflicted with brutality against women. In Engel's words, the challenge is to develop "a process by which the terrible *knowledge* carried by individual victims—knowledge that is so often isolating—would be transformed into public *acknowledgement* of the impact of sexual violence on our society."

Learning to Hold Our Hurt

The alchemy that transforms private grief into public healing demands we embrace the hurt. If we believe that depression is a sign of moral weakness we will try to hold off the pain. Or we will try to hold it down or hold it away. But how do we embrace pain effectively? Simply holding it up for everyone to see does not seem fruitful. Complaining endlessly seldom brings good results, since we neither face the problem nor find relief.

Our religious ancestors, too, flirted with unproductive grief. Stranded in the desert after escaping from Egypt, some of the people cursed Moses for their bad luck. Standing at the doors of their tents, they murmured against the leaders. But their grumbling did not have a target. These aggrieved tribesmen addressed neither Moses nor God directly. Instead they remained on the sidelines, muttering their complaints. Most gatherings today have members who excel in murmuring—repeatedly making complaints that never confront the problem nor help find solutions.

Holding our hurt in a certain embrace—neither keeping it out of view nor clutching it in futile complaint—initiates a process of healing. This saving dynamic does not magically absolve the pain or restore our loss. But depression's hold is broken. Theologian David Power describes the mysterious effect: "What is remembered in grief is redeemed, made whole, renewed."

Our ambulatory depressions are warning flares, alerting us to conflicts to be faced. To prevent this purge from degrading into punishment, we must learn to voice our pain and to hold our hurt. When we can do this, the prophecy of poet Robert Bly becomes true: "depression melts into grief" and healing begins.

Reflective Exercise

Everyday depression is an ordinary experience for most of us. But still, take care with this reflection, since for some of us "feeling blue" mushrooms easily into a lingering sadness. Start by recalling a recent time when you felt caught in an everyday depression—discouraged, defeated, tired. List some of the *thoughts* and *feelings* that were part of your gloomy mood.

Now, with the advantage of some distance from the experience, consider the context of this ordinary depression. What seemed to trigger your bad mood? Can you identify *threats* or *hurts* or *losses* involved? How did you respond: Blaming yourself or other people? retreating from contact? reaching out for help? Give some concrete examples of your attitudes and actions while you were depressed: What helped? what made things worse?

Finally, can you identify any ways in which this everyday depression served you well? Again, offer concrete examples.

Additional Resources

In *When Feeling Bad Is Good*, Ellen McGrath examines the sources of six "healthy depressions" and strategies for resolving them; see p. 22 for her definitions of healthy and unhealthy depressions and chapter 10 for her discussion of the types of unhealthy depression. On women's special vulnerability to this disorder, see the American Psychological Association report *Women and Depression: Risk Factors and Treatment Issues*, edited by Ellen McGrath, Gwendolyn Keita, Bonnie Strickland, and Nancy Russo.

D.W. Winnicott links the healthy experience of depression with mourning and the ability to feel guilt; see "The Value of Depression" in his *Home Is Where We Start From*. Robert Solomon explores the positive dynamics of depression in *The Passions*, pp. 294 and following. Robert Bly suggests the connection between depression and grief in *Iron John*; see p. 130. For a poignant personal account of severe depression, see William Styron's *Darkness Visible*. Donald Hall's observation about the effort to escape depression appears in his *Life Work*, p. 25.

Maggie Scarf examines depression in the lives of women in *Unfinished Business: Pressure Points in the Lives of Women*; for the quotations in this chapter see pp. 7, 85, 541, and 536. In *Silencing the Self*, Dana Crowley Jack stresses the influence of a "culture of inequality" on women who suffer depressive disorders; see p. 221. David Burns explores a range of practical strategies for overcoming debilitating patterns of distorted thinking in *The Feeling Good Handbook*.

David Power's observation on the power of grief appears in "Households of Faith in the Coming Church," *Worship* (May 1983), pp. 253–54; see also Walter Brueggemann's *Interpretation and Obedience*, p. 198. In *All Our Losses, All Our Griefs*, pastoral counselors Kenneth Mitchell and Herbert Anderson offer insight and practical resources for ministering to those caught up in grief. In his fiction and nonfiction writing, Holocaust survivor and Nobel Peace Prize winner Elie Wiesel shows us how to voice our pain in the noisy, sweaty prayer of lamentation; see, for example, *The Town Beyond the Wall*.

For summary statements of recent research on depression see Daniel Goleman, "If Hidden Depression Is Addressed, Patients May Recover More Quickly," *New York Times* (August 5, 1992) and "Childhood Depression May Herald Adult Ills," *New York Times* (January 11, 1994); Harold Schmeck, "Depression: Studies Bring New Drugs and Insights," *New York Times* (February 16, 1993); and Jane Brody, "Recognizing the Demons of Depression: The Pain May Be Disguised in Men," *New York Times* (December 18, 1991). An interview with anti-rape activist Barbara Engel appears in *The University of Chicago Magazine* (April 1993), pp. 30–33.

Conclusion

THE WAY OF THE NEGATIVE EMOTIONS

The Chinese character for The Way (Tao):
the mysterious path of befriending our emotions,
performing our passions, and
becoming fully human

The Way of the Negative Emotions

In the middle of the journey of my life
I found myself inside a dark forest, for
the right way I had completely lost.

Dante

Calamities befall us on the journey of our life but there is no other route to our destination. Journeys figure prominently in many religious traditions. The exodus and the exile define the spiritual journey for Jews. Pilgrimages—to Mecca or Jerusalem or Fatima—move religious seekers across varied landscapes. The ultimate question of every quest is "how do we get there from here?" Often, the question arises "inside a dark forest," when we realize "the right way I had completely lost."

Finding Our Way

The way of the negative emotions, like the Tao of Taoism, is a mysterious dynamic through which our life unfolds. The Tao is "silent, vast, independent and unchanging" (*Tao Te Ching*, 25). Clues, rather than clear road signs, mark the path. Attempting to plumb our passions, we set off on a trek without a finish line. If we endure, the way discloses harmful habits of our past and opens us to unexpected reservoirs of energy. The route is cyclic, winding repeatedly past familiar haunts but different at each passing because we have changed along the way.

Not everyone enters upon the mysterious way of the negative emotions; instead, we may linger in a life of quiet desperation, bound by boredom or hedged in by guilt. Conforming numbly to what is expected, we may never take leave, never launch out into the deep of our fathomless feelings.

When we do dare embark, we quickly detect the spiritual exercises required of us, especially those of presence and participation. Out of the "dark forest" we travel toward presence—becoming more attuned to the history that has molded our emotions and more aware of aspirations abandoned along the way. We bid farewell to the myriad techniques of distraction through which we had sought to absent ourselves from feeling. We journey, too, out of passivity toward participation. From the status of victims who bemoan our bad luck and dysfunctional families, we become actors in our interior life, acknowledging our complicity in the guilt or resentment we still harbor. Along the way, we begin to perform our passions, shouldering the risks of a life both passionate and responsible.

The way of the negative emotions leads us toward participation in a second sense. We are not lone players in a private drama, attempting a solitary and heroic healing. As we were injured by unwholesome environments, so we are healed by compassionate companions and healthy gatherings. The path of the negative emotions is a *way with*, a social adventure.

Stage One of the Journey

This book opened with the Chinese character for patience: a knife suspended over a heart. The way of the negative emotions begins with the courage to hold still long enough to recognize what we are feeling. Such patience is not a placid compliance, but a courageous attention to the turns and invitations of our life.

"A wild patience has taken me this far." Thus does poet Adrienne Rich describe her efforts to steer a course through the narrows of her life. "In this forty-ninth year of my life," she struggles to integrate the once conflicting energies of "anger and tenderness: my selves." To weave together life's disparate elements into a coherent story takes time and patience. To see our commitments through to fruition demands endurance.

Rich's patience is *wild*—not the passive submission that women, the poor, and minorities have been instructed in. The traditional virtue of patience earns a bad reputation where political and religious leaders

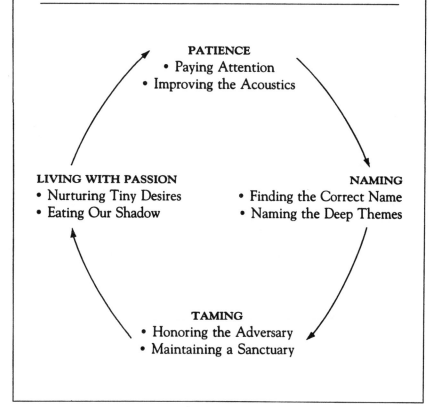

The Way of the Negative Emotions
A Journey Toward Presence and Participation

PATIENCE
- Paying Attention
- Improving the Acoustics

NAMING
- Finding the Correct Name
- Naming the Deep Themes

TAMING
- Honoring the Adversary
- Maintaining a Sanctuary

LIVING WITH PASSION
- Nurturing Tiny Desires
- Eating Our Shadow

encourage followers to submit to servitude and accept their fate. There patience is stripped of its courage and domesticated into docility. In her poem, Rich reminds us that finding our way through the mystery of our life is a demanding exercise.

To receive the surprising gifts of the negative emotions, we need much patience. We will have to *suffer* them actively and in full consciousness. We will have to feel as bad as we feel. Patience trains us to savor our life; tasting our painful emotions rather than simply swallowing them.

Paying Attention

The pain of a negative emotion gets our attention. Patience arrests our flight from feeling, helping us stay attentive. Ancient sages and contemporary social sciences agree on the value of this virtue. A central virtue in the Confucian moral armory was *ssü*: "attentive awareness." Confucius believed that nine aspects of human interaction demand our special attention; the eighth is "anger, for the difficulties it causes." The potentially dangerous emotion of anger must be carefully attended to. Arthur Waley, in his commentary on Confucius, observes, "we must think of *ssü* rather as *fixing attention* on an impression recently imbibed from the outside and destined to be immediately re-exteriorized in action."

For the sage Mencius, *ssü* was a matter of moral alertness. "If one attends (*ssü*), one achieves it; if one does not attend, one does not achieve it." Chinese scholar Lee Yearley defines *ssü* as "an inner ability to focus attention in a selective but concrete fashion." In his study of Mencius's vision of courage, Yearley links the skill of attention with nurturing *ch'i*—that physiological/spiritual energy that sometimes flowers in anger. If one pays no attention to this volatile source of energy, *ch'i* either withers into timidity or mushrooms into rage. Paying attention is a discipline that helps refine a person's vital energy into courage.

Complementing these Chinese convictions is Mihaly Csikszentmihalyi's research at the University of Chicago. In *Flow: The Psychology Of Optimal Experience*, he describes the experiences of work and leisure that make people feel most alive and give them "a sense of participation in defining the content of life."

At the core of peoples' experience of *flow*—feeling most alive and absorbingly engaged—is the phenomenon of attention. To enter the optimal experience of flow, people must concentrate in a special and enriching way. A person absorbed in climbing a rocky cliff gives all her attention to the moment. Distractions fall away and time stops. Wrapped in the present challenge, she enters the nourishing *flow* of the experience. Similarly the wood worker or potter gives rapt attention to his task. Fully concentrated on what he is doing, he enters into a focused, nourishing mood. A baseball player who finds himself in the middle of a hitting streak reports that he "is seeing the ball clearly." During this brief period he is able to bring all his attention to what he is doing, without allowing distractions to intrude. Utterly focused, he performs with uncommon excellence.

Two characteristics of this experience are especially noteworthy. Absorbed in work or play we are taken out of ourself, lost in an activity that deeply refreshes us. Second, in the midst of these activities, the feel of time changes. We no longer watch the clock or calculate a finish line. Instead, time rushes by (we look up from an engrossing book to find the morning gone) or comes to a stop (we have no sense of time passing).

We call this ability *paying* attention because it is neither spontaneous nor free. Paying attention is a learned discipline and a developed skill. The ability to focus our attention on painful feeling sets us on the way of the negative emotions. As attention attunes us to the turmoil in our heart, we become aware of its acoustics.

A Question of Acoustics

In the Greek language which has so influenced Western culture, *listening* and *obeying* share the same verbal root. In its most basic sense, obedience means not meek submission but careful listening. We cannot obey unless we first pay attention to what is being said. Patience and attention are ways that we listen to our life; they are modes of our obedience.

The Greek word for listening and obedience (*akouein*) also gives us the word *acoustics*. Acoustics refer to the factors in an environment that allow us to hear what is going on. Some buildings have acoustics that distort music and muddle public announcements. Some hearts, too, have bad acoustics; crackling static and the feedback of judgmental voices make it almost impossible to attend to one's experience. For such a life, being patient and paying attention will be difficult. To set out on the healing way of the negative emotions demands we improve the acoustics of our heart. Only by listening well can we honor the laments and invitations being sounded there.

Stage Two: Naming the Emotions

If the way of the negative emotions follows a Taoist path, it will be wary of names. "The Tao that can be expressed is not the absolute Tao; the name that can be named is not the absolute name" (*Tao Te Ching*, chapter 1). Names are as illusory as they are illuminative. Words like anger or fear suggest well-marked provinces of feeling but the geography of the soul is a wilder terrain. John Updike describes this wilderness:

> You land, it seemed to him, on the shore of your own being in total innocence, like an explorer who was looking for something else, and it takes decades to penetrate inland, and map the mountain passes, and trace the rivers to their sources. Even then, there are large blanks, where monsters roam.

We try to civilize this terra incognita with names, while we argue with one another what our words really mean. A character in Michael Ondaatje's novel *The English Patient* muses about this endless conflict:

> She had always wanted words. She loved them, grew up with them. Words gave her clarity, brought reason, shape. Whereas I thought words bent emotions like sticks in water.

Even though words may bend "emotions like sticks in water," the need to name our passions is urgent and universal. Our ancestors in ancient Greece and Rome used names to personify the forces of the heart. Startled by the beauty of a poem or melody, they judged a *muse* had assisted the artist. An exceptionally gifted person was thought to be possessed by a *genie*; such a person was named a *genius*.

But malevolent forces, too, invade the heart. When people became furious, our ancestors believed, an enraging spirit—a *fury*—had invaded them. The Christian Bible recounts stories of demoniacs—persons possessed by some destructive power. Negative emotions erupted in such people, turning them into savages. To control the demon, one had first to find its name. Jesus confronted a deranged person who had been chained among the tombs, demanding of the demon within him: "What is your name?" (Mark 5:9). When the demon had given up its name—"My name is Legion for we are many"—Jesus was able to cast out the harmful spirit. Muses, genies, furies, demons: powerful forces moving within us. Anger, guilt, shame, depression: volatile inner energies waiting to be named and tamed.

The discipline of naming our emotions offers a three tiered challenge. First, what is this disruptive feeling? Second, what assumptions lie concealed in the names we assign? Does *anger* already imply an unacceptable feeling? Does *lonely* carry an evaluation of inferiority? In this second discipline, we must identify the often hidden judgments accompanying the names we assign to feelings.

A third challenge concerns the origins of our emotions. We may know that we are angry, but have no idea why. We may feel ashamed of our body, but have no clue as to the source of this shame. Full naming includes awareness of the origins of our feelings. Consider the example shared with us by a friend.

> Last year while my wife and I were visiting my aging parents, I drove the four of us to a business appointment. My father was sitting next to me on the front seat when we started our return. Unfamiliar with the quickest route home, I asked my father if we should turn at the next exit. When he didn't answer I glanced over and he seemed either unconcerned or lost. As we drove past the intersection (where we should, in fact, have turned), I was overwhelmed with anger. Barely controlling my rage, I managed to drive us home by another route.
>
> When we arrived, I asked my wife to go for a walk with me and we tried to puzzle out my sudden, surprising anger. Why did I get so enraged? We replayed the scene: I had asked my father the way home and he didn't know. There it was! All my life my father has been the one who knows the way home; for me this is his very definition. I assumed this would always be so. And now, in his late eighties, he doesn't know the way home! An abyss had suddenly opened; one of the pillars of my security had suddenly collapsed. Consciously I knew I could find my way home. But the change in

my father still startled me. As we talked, my anger rapidly dissipated. I began to see I would have to release my father from this covert contract—that he must always know the way home. Together we would find our way—and now with less anger.

The way of naming our emotions is fraught with peril. We frequently fool ourselves by assigning the wrong name or naively believing that simply naming a mood brings its cure. Yet naming is the only way through the thicket of emotion. Humbly, allowing for mistakes and self-deception, we continue to name the feelings that surge through us. Naming our emotions we are less their victims, even as we surrender the fantasy of becoming their masters. Gradually bringing these feelings to light, we see what we must do.

Stage Three: Taming the Emotions

Negative emotions confuse and frighten us. If our feelings are "wrong", then surely we must master them. If emotions simply inflict pain, we should avoid them or at least numb ourselves to their injury. But if they offer both revelation and transformation, we will look for a more friendly means to tame their energy.

The central challenge in taming is to honor the adversary. We honor negative emotions by allowing ourselves to feel them and by taking the effort to name them. We honor disruptive feelings when we use their energy to support needed change. The arousals of guilt and anger, the distress of shame and even depression help purify our lives. As we saw in chapter 6, taming our emotions requires learning the disciplines that release their energy creatively. The way of the negative emotions takes us on the journey from arousal to action.

Maintaining Sanctuaries

A sullen husband, a screaming child, and a barking dog were finally too much. Maria told her teenage son to watch the baby and ran from the house. Two blocks away she slipped into the back of a dark, empty church. Protected by this solitary space, at last she could cry. Fear and anger and regret spilled out into the quiet space. Finally she could acknowledge to herself how bad she felt.

Religion has long provided sanctuary and safe haven in conflicted times. In medieval Europe, church buildings functioned as legal asylums in which a fugitive could find protection. In the 1980s Christian groups in the United States formed a sanctuary movement to protect political refugees fleeing oppression in Central America and elsewhere.

Sanctuary is a place of safety. An emotional sanctuary is, by design, a place that allows us to fully experience dangerous feelings. But just as words may distort emotions, sanctuaries can become places to hide. The rituals of a religious institution may provide us with a hiding place to avoid our painful feelings. Refusing the demanding tasks of naming and taming, we instead bask contentedly in the ready-made sentiments of empty ceremony.

To tame our negative emotions, we seek out sanctuaries where we can genuinely experience our feelings. Effective sanctuaries appear in many guises: the comforting quiet of a chapel, the privacy of a counselor's office, the safe shelter of a hospital room. We find haven in a support group's acceptance or in the solitude of confiding our thoughts in a personal journal. In the movie *A River Runs through It*, a father and his two sons go frequently to a nearby stream for fly-fishing. With little talk and much concentration, they occupy this privileged place together. During difficult times they bring their negative emotions to the river; it serves as their sanctuary.

The Warrior's Sword

In the protected space of a sanctuary, we undertake a second task of taming: learning to distinguish healthy from unhealthy sentiments. Is the guilt we feel authentic or the residue of a distorted idealism that we must move beyond? Is our fear a response to current danger or the scar of an unhealed wound from the past?

In chapter 8 we explored the Jungian metaphor of the warrior—an interior resource that guards the vulnerable boundaries linking us to other people. Poet Robert Bly points to a second resource, the sword that the warrior wields. Swords are dangerous but useful. In the hands of the healthy warrior, a sword cuts clean, severing authentic emotion from its distortions. The sword separates healthy shame from fear of sexuality; it severs anger from resentment and the lust for revenge. The sword's edge pares away the jealousies that clutter our heart. Only when we know the difference between healthy and unhealthy emotion, can we trust our instincts and dare to act passionately.

Stage Four: Living With Passion

If the way of the negative emotions has no finish line, it does have a goal: to live with passion. The arduous disciplines of patience, naming, and taming teach us to trust our instincts. Knowing the difference between vindication and vengeance, we can afford to feel our anger. Having faced depression and discerned our grief, we can allow ourselves to mourn. No longer poisoned by toxic shame, we can dare to trust our emotional response.

Trusting our own responsiveness enables us, in Bly's words, to "nurture tiny desires." Early in life, much energy goes into defending ourselves or accommodating to others' demands. In the crush of duties and distractions, we lose track of our own best desires—deep longings still too fragile to make a claim on us. Grounded in no authority other than our slender hopes and tentative dreams, these tiny desires lie buried under the busy agenda of job and family and civic life.

Decades later, a crisis or illness or loss brings us to a halt. In the pause, our gaze is altered. We recognize longings we have long ignored. We recall our early love of music; now at age fifty-five we want to learn to play a new instrument. But, of course, it's too late to take that up . . . or is it? Personal ambitions set aside, dreams forgotten for thirty years, return as hopes and hints for our future. In these fragile desires, we remember what we really want.

Bly quotes William James's observation about the power of these *wants*:

> [Our] wants are to be trusted . . . the uneasiness they occasion is still the best guide of [our] life and will lead to issues entirely beyond [our] present power of reckoning.

Our wants often fly in the face of a familiar, well-developed social character, the solid shape of our responsible public persona. "The uneasiness they occasion" reminds us of passions long ignored. As we tame our negative emotions, we dare to listen again to tiny desires that show the way to a passionate future.

Eating Our Shadow

Living more comfortably with passion helps us reconcile ourselves with our shadow. The metaphor of shadow refers, of course, to the underside of our personality. These are the conflicted humors and less than noble thoughts that we prefer to keep in the dark. Our shadow includes the petty jealousies, the habits of sarcasm, the taking delight in another's failure. The shadow is also the reverse side of our strengths. Good at initiating plans, we have difficulty following projects through to completion. Or we are able to see through unjust political structures quickly, but have little tolerance for anyone questioning our opinions or our motives.

Each of us casts a long shadow. Often we push these unsavory parts of ourself outward, projecting the dark outline of what we dislike in ourselves onto others. If we remain unaware of these projections, they cloud our relationships and encumber our life.

The shadow in us has its own history. In the energetic idealism and enthusiasm of youth, like Icarus we fly directly toward the sun. This assertive posture safely hides our shadow behind us. It is utterly out of our view as our eyes focus on the light ahead.

As we mature, the shadow swings out from behind us. Now the sun no longer blinds us. Out of the corner of our eye we catch sight of our shadow. From the angle afforded at mid-life we spot a somber outline that looks disconcertingly familiar.

In a season of depression the sun swings behind us, leaving us face-to-face with our shadow. Our faults and limitations loom large; we cannot lose sight of them. Our shadow stretches out in front of us, absorbing our attention and obscuring our path.

As we touch the wounds of anger or guilt or shame on the way to healing, we begin, in the imagery of Robert Bly, to "eat our shadow." More comfortable with our weaknesses, we can now consume what we had been projecting. More familiar with our faults, we have less need of earlier defenses. A mid-life executive recognizes that he has been successful precisely because he has been so driven. Working hard, he has pushed himself toward achievement and pushed others away. Now he notices the shadow of this strength—the compulsiveness of his life. Gradually he lets up on himself. He begins to eat his shadow.

A woman, troubled by guilt all her life, realizes she cannot tolerate feeling beholden to anyone. Every debt must be quickly repaid, every gracious gesture received must be countered by a gift given. To help her relinquish guilt's grip on her life, she consciously allows herself to savor her indebtedness, seeing now how it links her life to others. She, too, begins to eat her shadow.

Gradually we let go what we no longer need. Since our shadow is part of us, we cannot completely jettison it. But gathering it back into ourselves we find that our shadow, embraced, is strangely nourishing.

Holding Our Emotions

The way of the negative emotions returns us to the metaphor of embrace. Before starting on the way, control of our emotions and our world seemed imperative. But crossing the bridge of sadness we learned that "to follow Jesus [is] not to change the world but to embrace it." Gradually we let go our ambitions of mastery, learning that losing control—as the Gospel predicted—brings us surprising gains. In the words of Roberto Unger:

> You lose the world that you hoped vainly to control, the world in which you would be invulnerable to hurt, to misfortune, and loss of identity, and you regain it as the world that the mind and the will can grasp because they have stopped trying to hold it still or to hold it away.

Pledged to a God of desire, we do well to return to Scripture to taste again Yahweh's anger and compassion, Jesus' disappointment and joy. Here we learn again how to hold the negative emotions, patiently in touch with the mystery that transforms our troublesome feelings into fruitful passions.

Reflective Exercise

In a final exercise, we invite you to consult your own journey. Begin by spending a few moments reflecting prayerfully on the figure The

Way of the Negative Emotions that appears on p. 176. Don't force any consideration; just hold yourself present to the chart.

Now consider an emotion that is sometimes troublesome for you. It may be one of the four we have considered here: anger, shame, guilt, or depression. Or it may be another feeling that is problematic for you these days. Once you have made your selection, trace that emotion through the disciplines of the Way.

Start with the discipline of *patience*. For example, have you gotten better at paying attention to the troublesome feeling when it arises? What helps you do this? How have you improved the acoustics in your heart? Don't rush the reflection. Other questions or insights may come on your own, helping you sense what *patience* means to you.

Then move on in a similar fashion to the other disciplines: *naming*, *taming*, and *living with passion*. Spend time with each, exploring what your past experience has been, what new hope you have now. Move at your own pace; completing the chart at one sitting is less important than savoring the realizations that are significant for you.

Bring the reflection to a close with a prayer of praise or gratitude or lament. When time allows, return to this exercise later with another emotion as your focus.

Additional Resources

Adrienne Rich's poem "Integrity" appears in her book *A Wild Patience Has Taken Me This Far*; see p. 8. Thomas Moore examines the spiritual journey with gentleness and depth in *Care of the Soul*; a Jungian psychologist, he returns often to the theme of the shadow. Margaret Frings Keyes discusses emotions in terms of the categories of the Enneagram in *Emotions and the Enneagram: Working through Your Shadow Life Script*. In *The Wisdom of the Ego*, George Vaillant demonstrates the positive function of the mind's defenses, which "like the body's immune mechanisms, protect us by providing a variety of illusions to filter pain and to allow self-soothing" (p. 1).

Doris Donnelly suggests exercises, rooted in Scripture and tradition, to nourish us on the way in *Spiritual Fitness: Everyday Exercises for Body and Soul*. Peter Campbell and Edwin McMahon offer the practical discipline of focusing as a way to befriend troublesome emotional experience; see their book *Bio-Spirituality: Focusing as a Way to Grow* and the video series *Spirituality and Focusing* and *Focusing Companions*.

Dierdre Davis Brigham discusses the interplay of emotions as mind-body interaction in *Imagery for Getting Well: Clinical Applications of Behavioral Medicine*. Piero Ferrucci provides a series of useful reflective exercises, drawn from the discipline of psychosynthesis, in *What We May Be*. In *The Healing Imagination: The Meeting of Psyche and Soul*, Ann and Barry Ulanov describe the imagination's vital role in spiritual living.

Robert Bly explores the function of the warrior's sword in *Iron John*, p. 167. His evocative suggestions for "discovering tiny desires" appear on pp. 112 and 132; on p. 206 he considers "eating the shadow." In *Flow: The Psychology of Optimal Experience*, Mihaly Csikszentmihalyi defines "flow" on p. 4 and examines the role of attention on p. 54. The passage from John Updike appears in his short story "Baby's First Step" in the *New Yorker* (July 27, 1992), p. 24. The passage from Michael Ondaatje's novel *The English Patient* appears on p. 238.

The compelling phrase "to follow Jesus [is] not to change the world but to embrace it" is from the work of theologian Alex Garcia-Rivera in "Sacraments: Enter the World of God's Imagination," *U.S. Catholic* (January 1994), p. 9. Roberto Unger's final quote is from *Passion: An Essay on Personality*, p. 111.

Confucius's remarks on anger appear in Book 16, chapter 10 of his *Analects*. Arthur Waley comments on *ssü* in his translation of *The Analects of Confucius*, p. 45. On Mencius's understanding of *ssü*, see Lee Yearley's *Mencius and Aquinas*, p. 63. Mencius's observation is from 6a 15; see *The Works of Mencius*, translated by James Legge, p. 885.

Bibliography

All scriptural quotations are taken from *The New Revised Standard Version* (London: Collins, 1989), unless otherwise noted. JB indicates a quotation taken from *The Jerusalem Bible* (New York: Doubleday, 1968).

Albin, Rochelle Semmel. *Emotions*. Philadelphia: Westminster Press, 1983.

Angelou, Maya. Interview with Maya Angelou. In *Writing Lives: Conversations between Women Writers*, edited by Mary Chamberlain. London: Virago Press, 1988.

Aquinas, Thomas. *Summa Theologiae*. Latin text with English translation by the English Dominicans. New York: McGraw-Hill, 1963.

———. *The Treatise on the Virtues*. Translated by John Oesterle. Notre Dame, Ind.: University of Notre Dame Press, 1966.

Aristotle. *Nicomachean Ethics*. In *The Basic Works of Aristotle*, edited by Richard McKeon. New York: Random House, 1941.

Averill, James. *Anger and Aggression: An Essay on Emotion*. New York: Springer-Verlag, 1982.

———. "Six Metaphors of Emotion and Their Theoretical Extensions." In *Metaphor in the History of Psychology*, edited by D. Leary. Cambridge, U.K.: Cambridge University Press, 1990.

———. "Studies on Anger and Aggression: Implications for Theories of Emotion," *American Psychologist* (November 1983): 1145–60.

Bailey, F.G. *The Tactical Uses of Passion*. Ithaca, N.Y.: Cornell University Press, 1983.

Bateson, Mary Catherine. *Composing a Life*. New York: Penguin, 1990.

Bausch, Richard. *Rebel Powers*. New York: Houghton Mifflin, 1993.

Berkowitz, Leonard. "On the Formation and Regulation of Anger and Aggression." *American Psychologist* (April 1990): 494–503.

Bernardez, Theresa. "Women and Anger—Cultural Prohibitions." Work in Progress, No. 31. Wellesley, Mass.: Stone Center, 1988.

Bly, Robert. *Iron John*. New York: Addison-Wesley, 1990.

Borysenko, Joan. *Guilt Is the Teacher, Love Is the Lesson*. New York: Warner Books, 1990.

Bradshaw, John. *Healing the Shame That Binds You.* Deerfield, Fla.: Health Communications, 1988.

Brigham, Dierdre Davis. *Imagery for Getting Well: Clinical Applications of Behavioral Medicine.* New York: Norton, 1994.

Brown, Lyn Mikel, and Carol Gilligan. *Meeting at the Crossroads: Women's Psychology and Girl's Development.* Cambridge, Mass.: Harvard University Press, 1992.

Brown, Peter. *Body and Society: Men, Women, and Sexual Renunciation in Early Christianity.* New York: Columbia University Press, 1988.

Broyard, Anatole. *Intoxicated by My Illness.* New York: Clarkson Potter, 1992.

Brueggemann, Walter. *Interpretation and Obedience.* Minneapolis: Fortress, 1991.

Buckley, Thomas. "The Seven Deadly Sins," *Parabola* (Winter 1985): 6.

Burns, David. *Feeling Good.* New York: New American Library, 1981.

———. *The Feeling Good Handbook.* New York: William Morrow, 1989.

Callahan, Sidney. "Does Gender Make a Difference in Moral Decision Making?" *Second Opinion* (October 1991): 67–77.

———. *In Good Conscience.* New York: HarperCollins, 1991.

Campbell, Anne. *Men, Women, and Aggression.* New York: Basic Books, 1993.

Campbell, Peter, and Edwin McMahon. *Bio-Spirituality: Focusing as a Way to Grow.* Chicago: Loyola University Press, 1985.

———. *Focusing Companions* and *Spirituality and Focusing.* Kansas City, Mo.: Credence Cassettes, 1990. Audiocassettes.

Carmody, John. *Cancer and Faith: Reflections on Living with a Terminal Illness.* Mystic, Conn.: Twenty-Third Publications, 1994.

———. *How to Handle Trouble.* New York: Doubleday, 1993.

Clampitt, Amy. *Westward.* New York: Knopf, 1991.

Clement of Alexandria. *Le Pédagogue.* Edited by M. Harl. *Sources Chrétiennes,* vol. 158. Paris: Editions du Cerf, 1970.

———. "Stromata." In *Alexandrian Christianity,* edited by Henry Chadwick, vol. II. Philadelphia: Westminster Press, 1954.

Confucius. *The Analects of Confucius.* Translated by Arthur Waley. London: Allen & Unwin, 1983.

Csikszentmihalyi, Mihaly. *Flow: The Psychology of Optimal Experience.* San Francisco: HarperCollins, 1990.

Curran, Charles. *Faithful Dissent.* Kansas City: Sheed & Ward, 1986.

———. "Saul D. Alinsky, Catholic Social Practice, and Catholic Theory." In his *Critical Concerns in Moral Theology.* Notre Dame, Ind: University of Notre Dame Press, 1984.

Donnelly, Doris. *Putting Forgiveness into Practice.* 5th ed. Nashville: Abingdon Press, 1986.

———. *Spiritual Fitness: Everyday Exercises for Body and Soul.* San Francisco: HarperCollins, 1992.

Dowrick, Stephanie. *Intimacy and Solitude: Balancing Closeness and Independence.* New York: Norton, 1994.

Earle, Ralph, and Gregory Crow. *Lonely All the Time.* New York: Pocket Books, 1989.

Eichenbaum, Luise, and Susie Orbach. *Understanding Women: A Feminist Psychoanalytic Approach.* New York: Basic Books, 1983.

Ekman, Paul. "Facial Expression and Emotion." *American Psychologist* (April 1993): 384–92.

Erikson, Erik. *Identity and the Life Cycle.* New York: Norton, 1980.

———. *The Life Cycle Completed—A Review.* New York: Norton, 1982.

Erikson, Erik, Joan M. Erikson, and Helen Q. Kivnick. *Vital Involvement in Old Age: The Experience of Old Age in Our Time.* New York: Norton, 1986.

Erikson, Joan. *Wisdom of the Senses: The Way of Creativity.* New York: Norton, 1988.

Fairlie, Henry. *The Seven Deadly Sins Today.* Notre Dame, Ind.: University of Notre Dame Press, 1979.

Ferder, Fran. *Words Made Flesh: Scripture, Psychology and Human Communication.* Notre Dame, Ind.: Ave Maria Press, 1986.

Ferrucci, Piero. *What We May Be.* New York: Jeremy Tarcher, 1982.

Fossum, Merle, and Marilyn Mason. *Facing Shame.* New York: Norton, 1986.

Fowler, James. "Faith, Liberation and Human Development." The Thirkield-Jones Lectures. Gammon Theological Seminary, 1974.

Freeman, Lucy. *Our Inner World of Rage.* New York: Continuum Books, 1990.

Frost, William, and James Averill. "Differences between Men and Women in the Everyday Experience of Anger." In *Anger and Aggression,* by James Averill. New York: Springer-Verlag, 1992.

Garcia-Rivera, Alex. "Sacraments: Enter the World of God's Imagination." *U.S. Catholic* (January 1994): 6–12.

Gaylin, Willard. *Feelings: Our Vital Signs.* New York; Harper & Row, 1989.

———. *The Rage Within: Anger in Modern Life.* New York: Simon & Schuster, 1984.

Gazzaniga, Michael S. *Nature's Mind: The Biological Roots of Thinking, Emotions, Sexuality, Language and Intelligence.* New York: Basic Books, 1992.

Geertz, Clifford. *The Interpretation of Cultures.* New York: Basic Books, 1977.

Gilligan, Carol. *In a Different Voice.* Cambridge, Mass.: Harvard University Press, 1982.

Gilligan, Carol, N. Lyons, and T. Hammer. *Making Connections: The Relational Worlds of Adolescent Girls.* Cambridge, Mass.: Harvard University Press, 1990.

Goldberg, Carl. *Understanding Shame.* London: Aronson, 1991.

Hall, Donald. *Life Work.* Boston: Beacon Press, 1993.

Hankins, Gary, with Carol Hankins. *Prescription for Anger: Coping with Angry Feelings and Angry People.* New York: Warner Books, 1993.

Harper, James, and Margaret Hoopes. *Uncovering Shame*. New York: Norton, 1990.

Harrison, Beverly Wildung. "The Place of Anger in the Works of Love." In *Making the Connections: Essays in Feminist Social Ethics*, edited by Carol S. Robb. Boston: Beacon Press, 1985.

Hillman, James. *Emotions*. Evanston, Ill.: Northwestern University Press, 1992.

Hochschild, Arlie Russell. *The Managed Heart: Commercialization of Human Feeling*. Berkeley, Calif.: University of California Press, 1983.

Jack, Dana Crowley. *Silencing the Self: Women and Depression*. Cambridge, Mass.: Harvard University Press, 1991.

James, Muriel, and John James. *Passion for Life*. New York: Dutton, 1992.

Janeway, Elizabeth. *Improper Behavior: When and How Misconduct Can Be Healthy for Society*. New York: William Morrow, 1987.

———. *Powers of the Weak*. New York: Knopf, 1980.

John Paul II. *The Splendor of Truth*. (*Veritatis Splendor*). *Origins* (October 14, 1993).

Juergensmeyer, Mark. *Fighting Fair: A Non-Violent Strategy for Resolving Everyday Conflicts*. New York: Harper & Row, 1986.

Karen, Robert. "Shame." *The Atlantic Monthly* (February 1992).

Kaschak, Ellyn. *Engendered Lives: A New Psychology of Women's Experience*. New York: Basic Books, 1992.

Kaufman, Gershen. *Shame: The Power of Caring*. Rochester, Vt: Schenkman Books, 1985.

Keen, Sam. *Inward Bound*. New York: Bantam, 1992.

Keillor, Garrison. *Lake Wobegon Days*. New York: Viking, 1985.

Kelley, Kathleen, ed. *Guilt: Issues of Emotional Living in an Age of Stress*. New York: Crossroad, 1990.

Keyes, Margaret Frings. *Emotions and the Enneagram: Working through Your Shadow Life Script*. Revised Edition. Muir Beach, Calif.: Molysdatur Publications, 1992.

Kitayama, Shinobu, and Hazel Markus, eds. *Emotions and Culture*. New York: American Psychological Association, 1993.

Kundera, Milan. "The Hitchhiking Game." *Esquire* (April 1974).

LaCugna, Catherine Mowry, ed. *Freeing Theology: The Essentials of Theology in Feminist Perspective*. San Francisco: HarperCollins, 1993.

———. *God With Us: The Trinity and Christian Life*. San Francisco: HarperCollins, 1991.

Lazarus, Richard S. *Emotions and Adaptation*. New York: Oxford University Press, 1991.

Lee, Bernard. *Jesus and the Metaphors of God*. New York: Paulist Press, 1993.

Lee, John, and Bill Stott. *Facing the Fire: Experiencing and Expressing Anger Appropriately.* New York: Bantam, 1993.

Lerner, Harriet Goldhur. *The Dance of Anger.* New York: Harper & Row, 1985.

————. *Women in Therapy.* New York: Harper & Row, 1988.

Lewis, Michael. *Shame: The Exposed Self.* New York: Free Press, 1992.

Lilla, Salvatore. *Clement of Alexandria.* New York: Oxford University Press, 1971.

Lorde, Audre. "The Uses of Anger: Women Responding to Racism." In *Sister Outsider: Essays and Speeches by Audre Lorde.* Freedom, Calif.: The Crossing Press, 1984.

Lynd, Helen Merrill. *On Shame and the Search for Identity.* New York: Harcourt, Brace, 1958.

MacIntyre, Alasdair. *After Virtue.* Notre Dame, Ind.: University of Notre Dame Press, 1981.

————. *"Sophrosunē: How A Virtue Can Become Socially Disruptive."* In *Ethical Theory: Character and Virtue,* edited by P.A. French, T.E. Uehling, and H.K. Wettstein. Notre Dame, Ind: University of Notre Dame Press, 1988.

Malatesta, Carol Zander, and Caroll E. Izard, eds. *Emotion in Adult Development.* Beverly Hills, Calif: Sage Publishers, 1984.

Marcus Aurelius. *The Meditations.* Translated by G.N.A. Grube. Indianapolis: Bobbs-Merrill, 1963.

May, Gerald. *Addiction and Grace.* New York: HarperCollins, 1986.

McCormick, Richard. "L'Affaire Curran." *America* 154 (1986): 261–67.

McCormick, Richard, and Richard McBrien. "L'Affaire Curran II." *America* 163 (1990): 87–105.

McGrath, Ellen. *When Feeling Bad Is Good.* New York: Henry Holt, 1992.

McGrath, Ellen, Gwendolyn Keita, Bonnie Strickland, and Nancy Russo. *Women and Depression: Risk Factors and Treatment Issues.* New York: American Psychological Association, 1993.

McKay, Matthew, Peter Rogers, and Judith McKay. *When Anger Hurts: Quieting the Storm Within.* Oakland, Calif.: New Harbinger Publications, 1989.

McKenzie, John. "Anger." In *The Jerome Biblical Commentary,* edited by Raymond E. Brown et al. Englewood Cliffs, N.J.: Prentice-Hall, 1968.

McNeill, John. *Taking a Chance on God.* Boston: Beacon Press, 1989.

McNulty, Frank. *A Theology of Feelings.* Kansas City, Mo.: Credence Cassettes, 1992. Audiocassettes.

Mencius. *The Works of Mencius.* Translated by James Legge. New York: Dover, 1970.

Milhaven, J. Giles. *Good Anger.* Kansas City: Sheed & Ward, 1989.

Miller, Jean Baker. "The Construction of Anger in Women and Men." *Work in Progress,* No. 4. Wellesley, Mass.: Stone Center, 1983.

Miller, Jean Baker, and Janet Surrey. "Revisioning Women's Anger: The Personal and the Global." Work in Progress, No. 43. Wellesley, Mass.: Stone Center, 1990.

Mitchell, Kenneth, and Herbert Anderson. *All Our Losses, All Our Griefs.* Philadelphia: Westminster, 1983.

Moore, Robert, and Douglas Gillette. *King, Warrior, Magician, Lover.* San Francisco: HarperCollins, 1990.

Moore, Thomas. *Care of the Soul.* New York: HarperCollins, 1992.

Mouw, Richard J. *Uncommon Decency: Christian Civility in an Uncivil World.* Downers Grove, Ill.: Inter-Varsity Press, 1992.

Munro, Alice. "Open Secrets." *The New Yorker* (February 8, 1993): 90–93.

Nathanson, Donald L., ed. *The Many Faces of Shame.* New York: Norton, 1987.

———. *Shame and Pride: Affect, Sex, and the Birth of the Self.* New York: Norton, 1992.

Neusner, Jacob. *Vanquished Nation, Broken Spirit: The Virtues of the Heart in Formative Judaism.* New York: Cambridge University Press, 1987.

Ondaatje, Michael. *The English Patient.* New York: Vintage International, 1992.

O'Neill, Mary Aquin. "The Mystery of Being Human Together." In *Freeing Theology: The Essentials of Theology in Feminist Perspective*, edited by Catherine Mowry LaCugna, 139–160. San Francisco: HarperCollins, 1993.

O'Shaughnessy, Mary Michael. *Feelings and Emotions in Christian Living.* New York: Alba House, 1988.

Osiek, Carolyn. *Beyond Anger: On Being a Feminist in the Church.* Mahway, N.J.: Paulist Press, 1986.

Peck, Scott. *The Road Less Traveled.* New York: Simon & Schuster, 1978.

———. *A World Waiting to Be Born: Rediscovering Civility.* New York: Bantam, 1993.

Phillips, Adam. *On Kissing, Tickling, and Being Bored: Psychoanalytic Essays on the Unexamined Life.* Cambridge, Mass.: Harvard University Press, 1993.

Pieper, Josef. *The Four Cardinal Virtues.* Notre Dame, Ind.: University of Notre Dame Press, 1966.

Potter-Efron, Ronald, and Patricia Potter-Efron. *Letting Go of Shame.* San Francisco: HarperCollins, 1989.

Power, David. "Households of Faith in the Coming Church," *Worship* (May 1983): 237–255.

Rich, Adrienne. *A Wild Patience Has Taken Me This Far: Poems 1978–1981.* New York: Norton, 1981.

Richardson, Ron. *Family Ties That Bind.* Chicago: Self-Counsel Press, 1991.

Ricoeur, Paul. *The Symbolism of Evil.* Boston: Beacon Press, 1967.

Rieff, Philip. *Freud: The Mind of the Moralist.* New York: Doubleday, 1959.

Rohrer, Norman, and Philip Sutherland. *Facing Anger*. Minneapolis: Augsburg, 1981.

Rogers, Mary Beth. *Cold Anger: A Story of Faith and Power Politics*. Denton, Tex.: University of North Texas Press, 1991.

Rorty, Amélie Eksenberg, ed. *Explaining Emotions*. Berkeley, Calif.: University of California Press, 1980.

Scarf, Maggie. *Unfinished Business: Pressure Points in the Lives of Women*. New York: Doubleday, 1980.

Schell, David W. *Getting Bitter or Getting Better: Choosing Forgiveness for Your Own Good*. Meinrad, Ind.: Abbey Press, 1991.

Schillebeeckx, Edward. *Ministry: Leadership in the Community of Jesus Christ*. New York: Crossroad, 1981.

Schneider, Carl. *Shame, Exposure and Privacy*. New York: Norton, 1992.

Schulman, Michael, and Eve Mekler. *Bringing Up a Moral Child*. New York: Addison-Wesley, 1985.

Seligman, Martin E. *Learned Optimism*. New York: Knopf, 1990.

Sharansky, Natan. *Fear No Evil*. New York: Random House, 1988.

Sheehan, Neil. *A Bright Shining Lie*. New York: Random House, 1988.

Shorris, Earl. *Latinos: A Biography of the People*. New York: Norton, 1992.

Smedes, Lewis B. *Forgive and Forget: Healing the Hurts We Don't Deserve*. San Francisco: HarperCollins, 1985.

———. *Shame and Grace: Healing the Shame We Don't Deserve*. San Francisco: HarperCollins, 1993.

Sofield, Loughlan, Carroll Juliano, and Rosine Hammett. *Design for Wholeness: Dealing with Anger, Learning to Forgive, Building Self-Esteem*. Notre Dame, Ind: Ave Maria Press, 1990.

Solomon, Robert. *The Passions: The Myth and Nature of Human Emotions*. Notre Dame, Ind: University of Notre Dame Press, 1983.

Spohn, William. "Notes in Moral Theology: 1990." *Theological Studies* (March 1991): 69–87.

Stearns, Carol Zisowitz, and Peter N. Stearns. *Anger: The Struggle for Emotional Control in America's History*. Chicago: University of Chicago Press, 1986.

Stegner, Wallace. *All the Little Live Things*. New York: Penguin, 1991.

Stringfellow, William. "The Joy of Mourning." *Sojourners* (April 1982): 29–32.

Styron, William. *Darkness Visible: A Memoir of Madness*. New York: Vintage Books, 1992

Swinburne, Richard. *Responsibility and Atonement*. New York: Oxford University Press, 1990.

Tannen, Deborah. "The Power of the Yell." *New York Times* (January 14, 1994): 21.

————. *You Just Don't Understand: Women and Men in Conversation.* New York: Ballantine Books, 1990.

Tavris, Carol. *Anger—The Misunderstood Emotion.* New Edition. New York: Simon & Schuster, 1989.

————. *The Mismeasure of Woman.* New York: Simon & Schuster, 1992.

Thayer, Robert. *The Biopsychology of Mood and Arousal.* New York: Oxford University Press, 1989.

Thompson, Clarence. *Healing Emotions with Biblical Images.* Kansas City, Mo.: Credence Cassettes, 1990. Audiocassettes.

Thompson, Sarah. *Women and Anger.* New York: Springer, 1993.

Tournier, Paul. *Guilt and Grace.* New York: Harper & Row, 1985.

Trible, Phyllis. *God and the Rhetoric of Sexuality.* Philadelphia: Fortress Press, 1978.

Tyrrell, Thomas. *The Adventure of Intimacy: A Journey through Broken Circles.* Mystic, Conn.: Twenty-Third Publications, 1994.

Ulanov, Ann, and Barry Ulanov. *The Healing Imagination: The Meeting of Psyche and Soul.* Mahway, N.J.: Paulist Press, 1991.

Unger, Roberto. *Passions: An Essay on Personality.* New York: Free Press, 1984.

Updike, John. "Baby's First Step." *The New Yorker* (July 27, 1992): 24–27.

Vaillant, George. *The Wisdom of the Ego.* Cambridge, Mass.: Harvard University Press, 1993.

Villaseñor, Victor. *Rain of Gold.* New York: Dell Publishers, 1991.

Wechsler, Harlan J. *What's So Bad about Guilt?* New York: Simon & Schuster, 1990.

Weisinger, Hendrie. *The Anger Workout Book.* New York: Quill, 1985.

West, Cornel. *Keeping Faith: Philosophy and Race in America.* New York: Routledge, 1993.

————. *Race Matters.* Boston: Beacon Press, 1993.

Whitehead, Evelyn Eaton, and James D. Whitehead. *Community of Faith: Crafting Christian Communities Today.* Mystic, Conn.: Twenty-Third Publications, 1992.

Whitehead, James D., and Evelyn Eaton Whitehead. *The Promise of Partnership: A Model for Collaborative Ministry.* San Francisco: HarperCollins, 1993.

Wiesel, Elie. *The Town Beyond the Wall.* New York: Holt, Rinehart and Winston, 1964.

Williams, Bernard. *Shame and Necessity.* Los Angeles: University of California Press, 1993.

Williams, Redford, and Virginia Williams. *Anger Kills.* New York: Random House, 1993.

Wilson, James Q. *The Moral Sense.* New York: Free Press, 1993.

Winnicott, D.W. *Home Is Where We Start From.* New York: Norton, 1986.

Yearley, Lee. *Mencius and Aquinas: Theories of Virtue and Conceptions of Courage.* Albany: State University of New York Press, 1990.

Index

About the Authors

Evelyn Eaton Whitehead is a developmental psychologist. She holds the doctorate from the University of Chicago. Her professional work focuses on issues of adult maturity, the dynamics of leadership, and the social analysis of community life.

James D. Whitehead is a pastoral theologian and historian of religion. He received the doctorate from Harvard University. His theological interests concern questions of contemporary spirituality, religious leadership, and theological method in ministry.

The Whiteheads are consultants in education and ministry through WHITEHEAD ASSOCIATES, which they established in 1978. Their work serves religious-sponsored groups and other service organizations in the United States and abroad; they contribute regularly to programs of leadership development, adult formation, and health-care ministry.

The Whiteheads are Associate Faculty of the Institute of Pastoral Studies at Loyola University of Chicago, with which they have been affiliated since 1970. They served as Distinguished Visiting Professors at the Warren Center of the University of Tulsa in 1992. They currently make their home in South Bend, Indiana.